THERE MUST BE SOMETHING MORE

by

Luanne Jones Owensby

"Publish His glorious deeds...
Tell everyone about the amazing things He does."
(Psalm 96:3-NLT)

There Must Be Something More
© 2005 Luanne Jones Owensby

Cover photography by Bryan S. Owensby

Contributions will be made to ovarian cancer education and
awareness from the sale of this book.

DEDICATION

To Amelia, my sister by divine appointment. It was an incredible journey that ended much too soon. You taught us all so much about how to live, and how to die. The battle is over; the victory is won. To God be the glory; great things He has done. I love you, and I'll see you again soon!

To all the other ladies who are fighting this dreadful disease. May God send you a sister to be by your side on your journey. May you find the same faith, hope, love, strength, and courage that Amelia had. May you fight a good fight, finish the race, and keep the faith. May someone always be on the sidelines, cheering you on!

ACKNOWLEDGMENT

I am deeply indebted to my friends and family who encouraged and assisted me in completing this project. I am especially grateful for my sister, Susan, and my friend, Ginger, who worked so diligently on the editing of my manuscript. I also owe a word of gratitude to Benita, Jackie, and Marianne, who assisted in proofreading. This has been a source of healing for me, and I pray it will be an encouragement to others who find themselves on this journey they would never have chosen to take.

TABLE OF CONTENTS

INTRODUCTION

This is a true story about an incredible two and one-half year journey two women shared in a battle with ovarian cancer. They were strangers until this common thread stitched their hearts and lives together. It was not by accident or coincidence that they met. It was truly a part of God's perfect plan for their lives. They called themselves sisters by divine appointment.

This journey was actually to a very bad place they would never have chosen to visit. It was to a place called *Cancer.* Some of the brief stops along the way were to *Pain, Suffering, Discouragement*, and *Disappointment*. However, they chose to spend most of their time in places such as *Faith, Hope, Love, Strength,* and *Courage*. God had planned this trip. He promised He would not leave them nor forsake them, and indeed He did not. He was with them all the way!

– – – – – – – – – – – – – – –

Like any other journey you take with a friend, I was sad and disappointed when it came to an end. I sat alone wondering, "Where do I go from here?" Then God began speaking to me about sharing the experiences of this journey with others. When you have taken a trip of a lifetime, you don't return home and quietly keep all your experiences to yourself. You want to tell somebody! This is my attempt to tell somebody about my incredible, life-changing journey with Amelia, my sister by divine appointment.

≻Chapter One≺

THE UN-HAPPY VALENTINE'S DAY

It was February 14, 2002. I had taken off work for the day and was heading into downtown Atlanta with my husband. It could have been the setting for a wonderful Valentine's Day. It probably was the most memorable Valentine's Day I will ever have, but it was not a happy day. We were on our way to the office of a gynecologic oncologist. It felt like a nightmare I was sure to awaken from soon.

This nightmare had actually started about four weeks earlier. Some medical concerns had taken me to my local gynecologist. An ultrasound had revealed numerous large masses on both my ovaries. The technologist who performed this ultrasound appeared a bit perplexed. She told me not to worry, but she was going to call in another technologist to take a look. She had been unable to see either ovary on the screen that day. I wasn't overly concerned because this had happened before. I had taken a prescription medication (Provera), and another ultrasound had been performed a few weeks later. Each time, the masses had proven to be cysts that had ruptured, and everything was back to normal. Things would turn out differently this time.

After taking the usual medication for one week and waiting two more weeks, I returned for the second ultrasound. I was sure everything was going to be fine. Unfortunately, this time the masses were still there. Even worse, they were considerably larger than they had been three weeks earlier. My gynecologist told me that surgery was inevitable. I asked how soon he would schedule this and was not at all prepared for his response. He related that he would not want to go into surgery and find something he was not prepared to handle. He was referring me to a gynecologic oncologist in Atlanta. I could not have been more stunned. This was certainly not the news I had anticipated.

My gynecologist spent much of his time the next morning making arrangements for this visit to Atlanta. He was told that I could be worked in on an emergency basis later in the week if all the necessary paperwork and lab results could be completed. He assured them he would rush the lab results and even hand-deliver them if necessary. Because he was so adamant that I be seen quickly, I knew this was a serious matter. I spent three sleepless nights prior to my appointment that had been arranged for Thursday. My mind was running rampant. I knew that ovarian cancer is considered a "disease that whispers" and is fittingly called "the silent killer". The symptoms are vague. It is not usually detected with a routine pelvic examination and Pap smear. The cancer is usually more advanced and has invaded other organs before specific symptoms are noted. I checked the Internet to glean more information about ovarian cancer. I didn't comprehend everything I read, but one thing was very clear. I had every symptom that was mentioned!

My thoughts drifted toward my family. I tried to imagine my two children growing up without me being there for them. I thought about missing all those special times in their lives that every mother anticipates. How would I tell my family and friends? What would they say? What would chemotherapy involve? Would I be weak and nauseated? Would I lose my hair, and what would I look like? I had already decided that I would let my hairdresser shave my head and assist me in getting a nice wig.

On the morning of my scheduled appointment in Atlanta, I was at home alone for a few minutes. My husband had taken our children to school and was going to make a quick stop by his office before coming back for me. I sat down on the sofa in our family room with my Bible in my hand. I immediately sensed that I was not really alone. The presence of the Holy Spirit was so evident that I felt as though my Heavenly Father was sitting right next to me. I almost felt as though I could reach out and grasp His hand in mine. I was in need of His strength and encouragement for this day, because I was weak and afraid. Psalm 46:1 reminded me that *"God is our refuge and strength, A very present help in trouble."* My mind wandered back to my childhood days in Vacation Bible School, and I remembered one of the first Bible verses I ever learned. *"Whenever I am afraid, I will trust in You. In God (I will praise His word), In God I have put my trust; I will not fear. What can flesh do to me?"* (Psalm 56:3).

Like so many women, I try to handle things on my own if I possibly can. This was one time that I realized how hopeless and helpless I was to do anything about the present situation. I was trusting in Christ alone and His grace and strength to be sufficient for my needs that day. As I sat quietly on my sofa, I was led to my favorite chapter in the Bible. In Philippians 4:6-9, I was reminded to *"Be anxious for nothing, but in everything by prayer and supplication, with thanksgiving, let your requests be made known to God; and the peace of God, which surpasses all understanding, will guard your hearts and minds through Christ Jesus. Finally, brethren, whatever things are true, whatever things are noble, whatever things are just, whatever things are pure, whatever things are lovely, whatever things are of good report, if there is any virtue and if there is anything praiseworthy, meditate on these things. The things which you learned and received and heard and saw in me, these do, and the God of peace will be with you."* Later in that chapter, verse 19 assured me that *"my God shall supply all your need according to His riches in glory by Christ Jesus."* I then reminded myself that this was going to be one of those days when I would have to react on the basis of what I knew rather than how I felt.

Since I was being worked in on an emergency basis, I spent four long and agonizing hours in the oncology office that day. I made a quick observation about the other ladies in the waiting

9

room surrounding me. We all fit into one of three categories: those who had hair, those who had wigs, and those who had neither. I concluded that those who had hair also had very fearful and worried expressions on their faces. It was the same expression that I sensed was painted on my face. It was a fear of the unknown. One middle-aged lady looked terrified and fought back tears as she clung to her husband's arm. One young couple that we met had been married for less than one year and had been given the bad news. I still think of some of those couples and wonder how things turned out for them. There were women of all different ages, backgrounds, and interests in that room. We all shared one common fear: the fear that this silent killer had invaded our lives.

The gynecologic oncologist was a kind and compassionate man who tried to give me some words of encouragement that day. He was actually glad to hear that I was experiencing pain and discomfort and related to me that most of his ovarian cancer patients did not complain of pain on examination. He explained that this could possibly be a case of severe endometriosis, but emphasized the fact that he could not be certain of what we were dealing with until he got into surgery. He advised me that he would perform an exploratory laparotomy with total hysterectomy, bilateral salpingo-oophorectomy, and possible ovarian cancer staging. Biopsies would be evaluated during the surgery, and we would know immediately if they were malignant. He also wrote orders for me to obtain a CA-125 blood test, a CT of the abdomen and pelvis with contrast, and a chest X-ray. Surgery was scheduled for Monday, February 26.

I left the oncology office that day clinging to the one ray of hope I had been given. Actually, I was clinging to another hope I had been given long before that day. I also had a strong faith, trust, and hope in Jesus Christ.

Amidst the unknowns and uncertainties that I was facing, I did know for certain that I was not facing this battle alone. When we don't know what tomorrow holds, we can still know who holds tomorrow. While we were not sure what we would be facing, at least we now had a plan in place. Action was about to be taken. If it turned out to be bad news, the good news would be that we had discovered the problem and would be taking measures to resolve it.

I also felt that I was in good hands. I had been sent to a very reputable oncologist, and he had made a good first impression. Even more importantly, my Heavenly Father is the Great Physician, my provider and my healer. I could rest in the knowledge that He would hide me under the shadow of His wings (Psalm 17:8), just as a mother hen covers and protects her children. I could think of no better place to be at the moment.

➤Chapter Two➤

NO REASON TO DOUBT

The oncology office did an excellent job of handling all the necessary procedures and paperwork for approval with my insurance company. That can be a harrowing experience for a well person. I am sure they are aware that their patients are on stress overload and in no frame of mind to deal with insurance company issues. I had one week to return to work and get everything in order there so that I could be away for at least six weeks. Being an occupational therapist in the school setting, I had many special needs children on my caseload who would need to be reassigned to other therapists. That would be more than enough to keep me busy during my week of waiting.

I found that one of my most difficult tasks was simply telling my family and friends what I might be facing. I have decided that cancer is one of the ugliest words I know. I had a hard time even saying the word. I found myself referring to it as "the C word", "the bad stuff", or "malignant". I simply could not utter the word cancer. I did not want to tell my children yet and alarm them unnecessarily. I did call a few family members and friends who I trusted to be prayer warriors for me during this interim period. My pastor had gotten our bad news and called me at work the following morning to assure me of his prayers and concern. I told him that God had never failed me, and today would not be a good time to start doubting Him. In fact, I had no reason to believe anything less than a miracle would happen for me. I've heard of many stories of miracles and healings, but I have witnessed several incidences in my own immediate family.

In 1975, my father was diagnosed with a malignant melanoma. The dermatologist who diagnosed this called with the bad news on Thanksgiving Day and told us we were to be at an Atlanta hospital the next day. He was so concerned in getting immediate attention that he settled for a second choice hospital rather than wait for a bed at his preferred location. This was an indication to us of the seriousness of the situation. My dad is now 80 years old, and has never had a recurrence. I consider that a miracle!

In 1986, I began experiencing some hormonal and endocrinology problems. An MRI revealed a small tumor on the pituitary gland. It was situated between the optic nerves and could cause blindness if it continued to grow. There would be dangers involved in going in to this critical area if it became nec-essary to remove it. The tumor was ultimately diagnosed as a benign microadenoma, too small to require surgical removal. It has been easily treated and maintained with medication since the diagnosis was made. I consider that a miracle!

In 1989, my mother was found to have masses on both kid-neys. One kidney would have to be removed immediately, and we were told it was almost certainly malignant. In fact, we were also informed that since the kidneys are considered a filtering system for the body, this was probably not the primary site of the malig-nancy. Scans would be performed to determine the extent of the disease. We were extremely fearful and worried about the prog-nosis. After surgery and three long days of waiting for pathology reports, we were given unbelievably good news. My mother was actually the seventeenth person in recorded medical history to have had this type of problem and it not be malignant. Her doc-tors assured us that her case would certainly be documented in medical textbooks. I consider that a miracle!

In 1990, my dad had been having pain in his knee, and we became concerned that he might have a torn ligament. Test results revealed something much more serious. A tumor was noted on a bone just below the knee. My mind raced with all of the worst case scenarios. Being a therapist myself, I was thinking of how difficult it would be to get him up and ambulating again on a prosthetic leg. It would have been even worse to see a man who had been so active spend the remainder of his life in a wheelchair. Our local orthopedist referred us to a bone cancer specialist in Atlanta. We had taken our X-rays along with us that day. I felt as though we were walking into an office to be rendered a death sentence. The oncologist walked into the room and slipped the films onto the lighted screen. He immediately turned back to us and responded that we had absolutely nothing to worry about. He referred to this bone mass as a benign tumor that had probably been there since my dad was a small child. We had a joyful ride back home. I consider that a miracle!

In 2002, my teenage daughter had a dark spot and line to appear under a toenail. She had shown this to me, but we were not concerned until I read a magazine article about skin cancers. It specifically mentioned that a dark spot and band that runs along the length of the nail bed could be indicative of a melanoma skin cancer underneath the nail. Because of our family history of melanoma, I froze in fear. We immediately went in to see our local dermatologist who was also very concerned with what he saw. Results of a biopsy were inconclusive. We were then sent to a physician at a medical center in Atlanta who specializes in the treatment of melanoma. Another surgical procedure and biopsy were performed there. My husband and I were just a few days away from leaving on a two week mission trip to Europe. We had known very clearly that we were to be a part of this trip. My only two initial concerns had been leaving my two children a continent away, and the financial need that it would require.

Shortly after we began to pray about being a part of this team, my son was injured in a high school football game. The additional sports injury insurance policy I had taken for him one month earlier reimbursed us for this accident claim. It was exactly the amount that would be needed for the mission trip. We took that as a very clear sign that God was calling us and providing the means for this trip. We had been so confident in this until two weeks before we were to leave when this problem arose with our daughter. Satan seeks to destroy the great plans God has for our lives. His plan was to use this incident to bring fear and doubt, and make us lose our focus and change our God ordained plans.

Just three days before we were to leave for Europe, we received the phone call that all was well. This dark spot was actually just an area of increased pigmentation. The doctor related to us that if this had been left unaddressed, it certainly could have become something more serious. However, at the present time we could just consider that she had a freckle under the nail. I consider that a miracle!

These are just a few of the physical miracles I have seen in my immediate family. Miracles truly do continue to happen everyday. We just fail to recognize most of them for what they really are. The birth of a child into our family is certainly a great miracle. I suppose the greatest miracle that we witness today is the rebirth of a child into the family of God. *"And you He made alive, who were dead in trespasses and sins" (Ephesians 2:1).* We can also read the biblical accounts of the miracles Jesus Christ performed many years ago. The lame became able to walk, and sight was restored to the blind. Lepers were cleansed of their disease, and others were even raised from the dead. I reflected on these miracles that I had read about and observed in my own immediate family and rested in the knowledge that God continues to be all-powerful and unchanging. Therefore, I had no reason to doubt!

≻Chapter Three≺

WHAT A COINCIDENCE!

Three days before I was scheduled for surgery, I received a call from a dear friend. Patty said to me, "Luanne, you're never going to believe this, but a lady in our choir is having the same problems you are having. She went to the same local gynecologist that you were seeing and was given a similar report. He has referred her to the same gynecologic oncologist in Atlanta, and she will be coming up next week to see him." I was so engrossed in my own situation that I did not think much more about this lady until almost a week later. I spent those last three days preparing for surgery. On Friday, I began a special diet that became more restrictive each day. By Sunday morning, I could only have clear liquids. Sunday afternoon, I had to begin drinking one gallon of a liquid laxative that was called "Golightly". I soon decided the person who named this drink must be the master of cruel jokes.

I was admitted to the hospital early on Monday morning for surgery. As I sat in the Admissions Department that morning waiting to be called back to the surgical suite, I felt a sense of incredible calmness and peace. I sensed a strong presence of the Holy Spirit again. My husband was holding his Bible, and I asked him to reread Philippians 4. When we arrived in the surgical holding area, a nurse asked if I needed a shot to calm me. I responded, "No, I am fine. Let's just go do what we came here to do!" A friend came back for a second and told me that she was praying for a peace that passes all understanding for me that morning. A few minutes later, my pastor came back to have prayer with me. He also prayed for peace that passes all understanding. That was for me another reaffirmation that God was very near and at work in this situation.

I was soon taken into the operating room where I was still totally awake, and I moved myself over onto the surgical table. Seconds after the intravenous fluids were started, I was asleep. A large host of family and friends were in the waiting area to support, encourage, and pray for me. And yes, I did receive another miracle that day. Biopsy reports indicated that my problem was indeed severe endometriosis. Most of the rest of that day is a blur. I remember being taken to room 218 and asking my husband if everything was okay. Knowing all was well, I was able to rest peacefully for the remainder of the day.

The next few days in the hospital were rather routine days of recuperation. My husband stayed by my side throughout the hospitalization. He looked forward to his daily outing, which was a trip across the street to Chick-fil-A. One cold night he decided to take a second outing and stayed away too long. He had been locked out of the hospital! When he finally returned, warmed up, and related his adventure, I realized how good it felt to be able to laugh together again. We also got pretty good at walking the complete circle on the second floor while pushing an I. V. pole. That takes coordination skills we never realized we possessed. We woke up on Thursday morning, and it seemed unusually bright outside. We peeked out the window onto Peachtree Street to witness a beautiful snowfall that had been sent to us during the night. It was another gift from above that reminded us of God's mercy and compassion, so pure and fresh each day.

My oncologist came into my room early on Friday morning bearing good news. I was going home! There is truly no place like home. The hospital is the best place to be when you are sick, but home is definitely the place to be when you are feeling better. He shared with me and my husband about what a joy it had been for him to be able to give us good news. He rarely has that opportunity in his field of medicine. He also commented that I must have had lots of folks praying for me. He could not have been more accurate in that statement.

I was lying in bed waiting for all the necessary dismissal procedures to take place. For the first time during that week, I remembered Patty's phone call the Friday night before and thought about the lady from her choir who was coming in for surgery later that morning. As I was lying there in bed, I closed my eyes and began to pray for this lady. "Dear Lord, please be with Patty's friend today. I know what she is going through as she anxiously waits in Admissions for her name to be called and to be taken back for surgery. Please bless our doctor with wisdom from above today and use him as your instrument of healing. Help her to be anxious for nothing, and give her the peace that passes all understanding like I felt on Monday morning. Please keep her safe and give her and her family sufficient grace for every need today. Amen."

Shortly after I prayed that prayer, Patty and her friend, Donna, came into my room. They had come to sit with Amelia's daughter, Kim, during Amelia's surgery. I shared with Patty and Donna that I was praying for Amelia and asked them to please let me know how she was doing after surgery.

Patty called me at home that evening with another coincidence. Amelia had been placed in Room 218, my room. Amelia was lying in the bed I had been in earlier that day when I had offered up prayers on her behalf. Were all these events just a coincidence? Absolutely not! Some people say coincidences are God's way of remaining anonymous. I used to refer to them as pats on the back from God. However, a year earlier I had read with much interest a book by Squire Rushnell entitled *When God Winks*. He describes these coincidences as winks from God. He believes that these happenings are little messages to you on your journey through life, nudging you along the grand path that has been designed especially for you. His book deals with helping us to open our eyes to the amazing ways that a higher power has been working in our life, learning to use coincidences to enrich our life, and recognizing that winks from God guide us through

18

every aspect of life. I was so intrigued by this concept that not only was I becoming better able to recognize these winks from God when they occurred, but I was actually starting to watch for them, to anticipate them.

Were having the same medical symptoms, the same local gynecologist, the same oncologist, the same hospital, the same room, the same bed, and a common friend all a coincidence? Oh no, these were not coincidences. These were truly "God Winks". The hand of God had gone before us, orchestrating all these common events and every other aspect of our lives. Amelia and I did not know it at the time, we didn't even know each other at the time, but God had big plans for us. We were about to embark on an incredible, life changing journey together.

➤Chapter Four◅

BE STILL AND KNOW

In Psalm 46:10, we are reminded to *"Be still, and know that I am God."* We live in a busy, fast paced society. We often find that we have more jobs on our "to do" list than we have hours in the day to accomplish them. We have more thoughts racing through our mind than we can comprehend, yet God has instructed us to be still and hear His voice. This is another of the many lessons that I have been reminded of through this incredible journey. Sometimes, I just need to be still. Otherwise, I may fail to hear Him. Ralph Waldo Emerson once stated, "There are voices which we hear in solitude, but they grow faint and inaudible as we enter the world."

Scriptures implore us to hear the voice of the Lord. *"When He had called the multitude to Himself, He said to them, "Hear and understand" (Matthew 15:10). "And a cloud came and overshadowed them; and a voice came out of the cloud, saying, "This is My beloved Son. Hear Him!" (Mark 9:7).* Scriptures also remind us that there are dangers associated with failing to hear and heed the words of the Lord as He speaks. *"Hear, O heavens, and give ear, O earth! For the LORD has spoken: "I have nourished and brought up children, And they have rebelled against Me; The ox knows its owner And the donkey its master's crib; But Israel does not know, My people do not consider." Alas, sinful nation, A people laden with iniquity, A brood of evildoers, Children who are corrupters! They have forsaken the*

LORD, They have provoked to anger The Holy One of Israel, They have turned away backward. Why should you be stricken again? You will revolt more and more. The whole head is sick, And the whole heart faints. From the sole of the foot even to the head, There is no soundness in it, But wounds and bruises and putrefying sores; They have not been closed or bound up, Or soothed with ointment. Your country is desolate, Your cities are burned with fire; Strangers devour your land in your presence; And it is desolate, as overthrown by strangers. So the daughter of Zion is left as a booth in a vineyard, As a hut in a garden of cucumbers, As a besieged city. Unless the LORD of hosts Had left to us a very small remnant, We would have become like Sodom, We would have been made like Gomorrah. Hear the word of the LORD, You rulers of Sodom; Give ear to the law of our God, You people of Gomorrah" (Isaiah 1:1-10). Isaiah was actually describing the arrogance and ignorance of Judah in this scripture passage. Unfortunately, it also aptly describes the conditions we are facing today in our own country, as we have chosen to turn a deaf ear to the instructions of the Lord. *"Therefore I will number you for the sword, And you shall all bow down to the slaughter; Because when I called, you did not answer; When I spoke, you did not hear..." (Isaiah 65:12). "Behold, the days are coming," says the Lord God, "That I will send a famine on the land. Not a famine of bread, Nor a thirst for water, But of hearing the words of the LORD" (Amos 8:11). "Therefore take heed how you hear. For whoever has, to him more will be given; and whoever does not have, even what he seems to have will be taken from him" (Luke 8:18).* During those times that we clearly hear His voice, we still have a choice in whether we will heed His instruction. The consequences of our choice can be far reaching. Consider the familiar story of Adam and Eve. God had placed them in the garden of Eden and had given them some very specific instructions. They both clearly understood that they could eat the fruit of any tree in the garden except from the tree of the knowledge of good and evil. However, the serpent approached Eve and was successful in

21

convincing both of them to disobey God's command. *"So when the woman saw that the tree was good for food, that it was pleasant to the eyes, and a tree desirable to make one wise, she took of its fruit and ate. She also gave to her husband with her, and he ate" (Genesis 3:6).* Unfortunately, Adam and Eve chose to disobey God's instructions, and all of mankind has suffered from their wrong choice.

Recognizing the voice of God is not always easy. However, the benefits of learning to do so are unlimited. The story of Eli and Samuel validates the importance of having a listening heart. Young Samuel knew about God, but had not yet experienced a personal encounter with Him. God had clearly spoken to Samuel twice already, and Samuel had thought that it was Eli who had called him. *"And the LORD called Samuel again the third time. So he arose and went to Eli, and said, "Here I am, for you did call me." Then Eli perceived that the LORD had called the boy. Therefore Eli said to Samuel, "Go, lie down; and it shall be, if He calls you, that you must say, "Speak, LORD, for Your servant hears." So Samuel went and lay down in his place. Now the LORD came and stood and called as at other times. "Samuel! Samuel!" And Samuel answered, "Speak, for Your servant hears." Then the LORD said to Samuel: "Behold, I will do something in Israel at which both ears of everyone who hears it will tingle" (I Samuel 3:8-11).* Samuel's willingness to hear and obey the instruction of God was rewarded. *"So Samuel grew, and the LORD was with him and let none of his words fall to the ground. And all Israel from Dan to Beersheba knew that Samuel had been established as a prophet of the LORD (I Samuel 3:19-20).* As is true in any relationship we build, His voice will become more discernable as we spend time with Him.

I have frequently thought of how differently things could have turned out in my journey with Amelia if some people had not been following this directive to be still and hear the voice of the Lord. The entire scenario could have been played out so differently, or not have occurred at all. So many people would have missed such rich blessings. My friend, Patty, is one of the busiest ladies I know. In addition to being music director at her church, she has a large number of piano students and is often called to assist with music for weddings, funerals, and other events. Her typical day starts early and ends late. She always has a sweet, joyful spirit and obviously finds time during her hectic day to be still and know that God is speaking. God spoke to Patty and revealed to her that she should call and tell me about her friend, Amelia. It was a great plan, but Patty could have caused it to be interrupted.

The same scenario could have transpired on my end of the situation, and God's plan could have again been interrupted. Patty could have followed through by calling me, but I could have whispered a quick prayer for her friend and gone on with my life. I could have gotten busy with other things and just never gotten around to following through with my good intentions. It is probably a good thing that I had doctor's orders to be still. Otherwise, I might have missed blessings untold. I have tried to imagine how differently my life would be now if I had never taken the journey with Amelia. I would probably have spent my six weeks recuperating, returned to work, gotten back into my usual routine, and thought little more about how blessed I was to have been spared the dreaded diagnosis of cancer. Amelia became a daily reminder to me of how incredibly blessed I had been to be spared what she was now facing.

God desires to commune and communicate with us. In I Peter 5:7, we are encouraged to cast all our care upon Him, because He cares for us. However, many of us spend far too much time talking to God rather than talking with God. By the time we have finished sharing our wants and plans with Him, we have little time left to listen to His desires and plans for us. An effective prayer life must include a time of silence before God. Prayer is like a phone call or a two-way conversation. It is more important that we listen than that we speak. When we speak, we are only repeating information that we know. When we are listening, we may acquire new information that will be helpful to us. It has been said that we have two ears and only one mouth. Therefore, we should listen twice as much as we speak. James 1:19 reminds us that every man should be *"swift to hear, and slow to speak."* The best way to really get to know someone and build a relationship is to spend time with them. It is vitally important that we spend time each day praying and reading God's word so that we build a relationship with Him and learn to recognize His voice. *"To him the doorkeeper opens, and the sheep hear his voice; and he calls his own sheep by name and leads them out. And when he brings out his own sheep, he goes before them; and the sheep follow him, for they know his voice. Yet they will by no means follow a stranger, but will flee from him, for they do not know the voice of strangers" (John 10:3-5).* God is often speaking, but we are not listening, or fail to recognize His voice. Sometimes we are hearing, but not understanding. Hebrews 5:11 speaks of those who have become dull of hearing. We have the capability of conditioning ourselves to ignore certain sounds, such as the early morning alarm clock. Some spouses have been accused of this selective hearing.

God has many different ways of getting our attention. We find numerous accounts in the scriptures of how God spoke to His people during those times. In Genesis 15:1, *"The word of the Lord came to Abram in a vision."* Exodus 3:1-4 gives the account of Moses tending a flock when *"the Angel of the Lord appeared to him in a flame of fire from the midst of a bush."* God had gotten the attention of Moses. When He turned and called to him, Moses said, *"Here I am."*

The Angel of the Lord spoke to Gideon. In Judges 6:17-22, we find Gideon's response in his moment of weakness. *"Then he said to Him, If now I have found favor in Your sight, then show me a sign that it is You who talk with me."* Like Gideon, we long to be given a clear sign, or expect God to speak in an audible voice so that we can be sure it is truly Him speaking to us.

God got the attention of Isaiah by shaking the foundations of the building and filling the room with smoke. After these happenings, Isaiah 6:8 states, *"Also I heard the voice of the Lord, saying: "Whom shall I send, and who will go for Us?" Then I said, "Here am I! Send me."*

God chose to use a blinding light to get the attention of Saul as he was traveling on the road to Damascus. Acts 9:1-9 gives the account of Saul as he fell to the ground and heard the voice of the Lord speaking to him. In verse 6, Paul was trembling and astonished and said, *"Lord, what do You want me to do?"*

Jesus was walking by the sea of Galilee one day when He noticed two brothers fishing. In Matthew 4:19-20, He said to them, *"Follow Me, and I will make you fishers of men."* They immediately left their nets and followed Him. Even in those times that we hear the voice of the Lord speaking to us, do we immediately drop what we are doing to obey Him?

God does continue to communicate with us today in various ways. I do not know of anyone personally who has seen a burning bush or a blinding light. However, I do know that He speaks by the Holy Spirit that indwells every believer as we read His word and pray. I also believe that He uses other people and situations we encounter to speak to us as well. When He speaks, what will our response be? Will we respond as Isaiah and say, "Here am I! Send me," or will our response be as the people to whom Isaiah had been sent to minister? God already knew that these people would not be receptive to His message and would remain unrepentant. In Isaiah 6:9-10, His command to Isaiah was to *"Go, and tell this people: Keep on hearing, but do not understand; Keep on seeing, but do not perceive. Make the heart of this people dull, And their ears heavy, And shut their eyes; Lest they see with their eyes, And hear with their ears, And understand with their heart, And return and be healed."*

Unfortunately, I am afraid that our response is not always the correct one. I fear that there are times when our worldly distractions cause us to hear but not understand and see but not perceive. Perhaps there are times when we are too busy to even see or hear at all. I believe God is very near and constantly speaking to us. We may fail to hear His voice or become too busy with other things on our agenda to respond to what God has asked us to do. Either of these things could have happened the day God spoke to

Patty, and the incredible journey would have just been another of God's great plans that never came to be.

As a pediatric occupational therapist, I work daily with children who are hearing impaired, visually impaired, or experience sensory and motor skill delays for various reasons. The sensory system has a profound impact upon good motor skill development. It provides valuable information and feedback about how we should respond and perform with our motor system. Consequently, an impaired sensory system can negatively impact a person's ability to respond motorically and impede normal growth and development.

Most of us are hardly aware of our sensory system unless we see a bright light, hear an unbearably loud noise, touch a hot stove, or smell a noxious odor. Consider the leprosy patient and you will have a better understanding of the profound impact an impaired sensory system can have on our ability to function. Leprosy causes lesions to develop on the skin. The disease progresses and causes peripheral nerve damage in the extremities. Consequently, there is sensory loss to the skin and weakness in the muscles. These victims may lose the function of their hands and feet, or may even lose an extremity, because of repeated injury they incur from the absence of sensation to these areas.

In my workplace, I frequently see the negative impact an impaired sensory system can have on a child's ability to learn and function independently. In the therapeutic setting, we provide opportunities for our special needs children to exercise their sensory and motor systems with the goal being to achieve normal growth and development. Measures are taken to assist our children with sensory processing or attention deficit disorders to stay focused, so they do not miss important information being presented to them.

Just as we all have physical senses, I believe we have spiritual senses. Scriptures implore us to exercise these spiritual senses for normal spiritual growth and development. *"Hear, you deaf; And look, you blind, that you may see"* (Isaiah 42:18). *"If anyone has an ear, let him hear"* (Revelation 13:9). *"My sheep hear My voice,* and I know them, and they follow Me" *(John 10:27)*. Psalm 34:8 encourages us to *"taste and see that the Lord is good."* We are reminded of the profound impact the touch of Jesus had on the woman with the issue of blood, the lame, and the blind who were brought to Him. We must strive to develop a keener sensitivity in our heart to recognize God's voice when He speaks and readily follow His instructions. May our prayer daily be that we would find time to be still and that God would sharpen our spiritual senses so that we might see His hand at work in our lives, feel His presence within us, hear His voice more clearly as He speaks to us, and follow the command that He gives to us. We should follow young Samuel's lead each day and say, "Speak, for thy servant heareth." As He speaks to us and we recognize His voice, may we respond like Paul and ask, *"Lord, what would you have me do?"* Our daily desire should be to know and do the will of God. *"Set your mind on things above, not on things on the earth" (Colossians 3:2).* May we never become so spiritually inattentive that we lose our focus on Christ and His perfect plan for our life. May we never become so busy that we miss a blessing, or deprive someone else of a blessing God had planned for them.

I recently heard someone say, "Amazing things happen when God shows up!" I pondered that thought for a while. I would propose that God does not have to show up; He is already with us. He is capable of being in all places at all times. *"...I am with you always, even to the end of the age" (Matthew 28:20). "...I will never leave you nor forsake you" (Hebrews 13:5). "Where can I go from Your Spirit? Or where can I flee from Your presence? If I ascend into heaven, You are there, If I make my bed in hell, behold, You are there. If I take the wings of the morning, And dwell in the uttermost parts of the sea, Even there Your hand shall lead me, And Your right hand shall hold me" (Psalm 139:7-10).* Perhaps a more accurate statement might be, "Amazing things happen when God's people listen up!"

How grateful I am that Patty took time from her busy day to hear the voice of the Lord and obey His instructions. How grateful I am that God spoke to me as I sat at my computer that

Wednesday night before I went to visit Amelia for the first time. I am so thankful that I heard His voice so clearly as He challenged me to become an encourager for Amelia. Otherwise, I would have missed blessings untold.

># Chapter Five ≺

THE DIVINE APPOINTMENT

My recuperation at home was going well, and each day I was moving around more easily and gaining strength. I was scheduled to return to my oncologist on Thursday to have those 32 staples removed! On Wednesday afternoon, I received another call from Patty. Amelia was not recuperating as quickly as they had hoped, and she was still in the hospital. Patty thought that perhaps I could give her a call of encouragement since I could better relate to what she was experiencing. I responded that I could actually do better than that. I told Patty that I would be going back to the hospital the next morning, and I would just drop by my old room and meet Amelia.

After hanging up the phone, I pondered over the commitment I had just made. It is not typically my personality to venture into a situation like this to meet a total stranger. Realizing I knew nothing about this lady, I wondered if she would appreciate me dropping in at such a difficult and emotionally vulnerable time. What would I say to her and how would she respond? I decided it might be a good idea to take along a card to leave with her. My family had left me alone for a couple of hours to attend Wednesday evening church activities. I sat down in our study and pondered what I should say to a lady who had just been given the devastating news that she did indeed have Stage III-C ovarian cancer.

I believe that God is always very near and speaks to us often. As I sat alone that night, there seemed to be no distractions. The presence of the Lord was very near as I sought His guidance in how I might be used to minister to this lady. I began to recall scriptures of faith, hope, and encouragement that I believed I should share with Amelia. I turned to my computer and began to put my thoughts into words...

March 6, 2002

Dear Amelia,

Although I have never met you, I feel as though I already know you. From talking with our mutual friend, Patty, it seems as though we have much in common. Because of this, you have been on my heart and mind daily for the past week. I'm sure you can relate well to the anxiety and fear that I felt when I was told I was facing surgery that my local gynecologist feared he might be unable to handle, and was sending me to an oncologist. I almost fell off the treatment table! I spent three anxious days and sleepless nights before going to see the gynecologic oncologist on Thursday. On Thursday morning before I left home, I sat quietly listening and talking to God. He led me to the fourth chapter of Philippians. There He reminded me to be anxious for nothing, but in everything by prayer and supplication, with thanksgiving, to let my requests be made known to God. He also reminded me that the peace of God, which surpasses all understanding, would guard my heart and mind through Christ Jesus. This was such an encouragement to me as I faced that day. While the oncologist was able to give me some encouragement about my situation, he did tell me that he wouldn't know for sure until he got in surgery exactly what we were facing. Nevertheless, God gave me a calm spirit, a peace that did pass understanding. On the Monday morning of my surgery, the nurse asked me if I needed something to calm me down, and I answered honestly, "No, I'm fine. Let's just go do what we need to do!" My husband and I had read again Philippians 4 as we waited in Admissions. Then my pastor arrived and prayed that I would have a peace that passes all understanding. Another friend came back to pre-op and shared that she had been praying that I would have perfect peace and calmness. God is so sufficient for our need! I believe you came to see the oncologist on the afternoon of my surgery. I mentioned you and our mutual friend when he made rounds the next morning. Then of course, you had your surgery the day that I finally got to come home. We both know well what you have to do to earn that status! Who would ever have dreamed you'd be stuck in a hospital until you could perform such a previously simple task?

Friday was a great day for me because I did get to come home. However, I just want to tell you how much you were on my mind Friday a.m. I knew you'd be arriving at Admissions, waiting to be called back, on to pre-op, and then surgery. I knew exactly what you would be going through, and I lay in my bed and I prayed that God would give you the peace that I had felt, and would go with you where no one else could go that day. It wasn't until that night when Patty called me at home that I learned you were lying in that same bed! I don't believe that was coincidence. I believe that was the hand of God at work, going a step ahead of you and working out some of the plans He has for your life.

I feel so unworthy of God's greatness in my life. I did get a good pathology report, and I praise him so much for this undeserved goodness to me. Because of this, I want to tell you that my recovery will be quicker, and I am committing myself to intercede for your quick and complete recovery. I look at this situation in my life as being similar to a race. You are running the same race a few days behind me, and I should finish the race a little ahead of you. You will have some extra hurdles to jump, but as soon as I finish my race, I am going to stand on the sidelines and cheer you on to your victory.

After leaving the doctor's office on Monday, I returned to my desk on Tuesday morning and my eye immediately went to a small plaque on my desk. It says: " Trials are not enemies of our faith, but opportunities for God to prove His faithfulness." He's been faithful to me, and I know He will be to you also. "Through the

31

Lord's mercies we are not consumed, Because His compassions fail not. They are new every morning; GREAT IS YOUR FAITHFULNESS" (Lamentations 3:22-23).

God's word and His presence in my life have truly been a lamp unto my feet and a light unto my path (Psalm 119:105) in this latest race I've had to run. I know it will be for you also. Meanwhile, please know that you will be in my thoughts and prayers.

In Christ,
Luanne

I folded this letter and placed it inside a card of encouragement I had chosen. As I sat there and held this envelope in my hand, God spoke to me very clearly. I can remember two incidences where I have heard God speak to me so clearly that it was almost audible. This was one of those times. He said that I would be an encourager for Amelia, that I would walk by her side on this journey, and help her make it through this difficult situation she was facing.

I am grateful that I was free of those typical distractions that might have interfered with my ability to hear God speak so clearly that night. I sat there and wondered how many other times God may have spoken to me, but I failed to hear His voice because of distractions. I wondered how many great blessings I may have missed because I had been too busy to hear from God. I dropped the envelope into my bag. I had received a clear command from God. I had a mission to accomplish.

I was anxious to get up and on my way to the doctor appointment that Thursday morning. I was excited to be getting all those staples removed and to be reassured that all was going well. I didn't realize it at the time, but I had another important appointment that morning: a divine appointment!

My husband and I made it through Atlanta traffic unusually easily that morning. We arrived at the hospital twenty minutes before my scheduled appointment, so I knew I had time to go by

Room 218 before I saw the doctor. I was obviously moving faster than I had since surgery because my husband commented on the way through the hospital about how fast I was walking. He didn't know it, but I was on a mission. I had heard a call from God the night before, and I was answering that call.

I arrived at the room and tapped on the door, which was already slightly opened. Amelia was lying in bed and said, "Are you Luanne? Patty called to tell me you were coming." I walked over to her bedside, and she reached out for my hand. I leaned across the bed, and as our arms embraced, our hearts united. Just as a mother experiences that special bonding when she touches her newborn for the first time, a special bond occurred between two ladies in Room 218 that Thursday morning. Little did we know that we were about to embark on an incredible journey together.

We talked for a moment or two about all the things we shared in common. She then remembered that another friend of hers had also been in that same room when she had surgery several years earlier for breast cancer. She told me that our doctor had been by earlier that morning and had given her the good news that she would be discharged. She was so excited to be going home and was anxiously awaiting her daughter's arrival to take her back home. Once again, God's timing had been perfect. We had managed to maneuver through Atlanta's morning traffic and get to the hospital before my appointment, and before Kim arrived to take her mom home.

I told her I had to go so I could get to my scheduled appointment. I reached into my bag and handed her the card I had prepared for her the night before. I held her hand again and assured her I was praying for her and believed she was going to be all right. She responded, "I think so, too!" I began to pray for Amelia daily and gave her a call at home the next week. She would be waiting for several weeks to recover from surgery before beginning chemotherapy.

The next time I saw her was in April at the hat party. She had begun her first of six chemotherapy treatments and was already losing her hair. The ladies in her church choir planned this party for her, and Patty had called and asked me to be the surprise guest that day. When Patty escorted me into the room, Amelia was so surprised and touched that I would have come that far, a 45 minute drive, just to be there for her. She stood up to hug me and asked, "Did you come just for me?" As we embraced, I was reminded of the first time I had leaned over her bed to give her a hug. I felt that special bond again, as I remembered and reaffirmed my commitment to be there for her.

Patty shared our story with the other ladies of how we had undergone the same surgery one week apart and how our similar situations had brought us together. She had not explained to them that my diagnosis had turned out very differently than Amelia's. I knew they must all be thinking I had either not started chemotherapy, or had on the best looking wig they had ever seen. I felt that I should share the happy ending of my story in the form of a praise to God for the great thing He had done in my life. However, a sense of guilt swept over me as I thought of how blessed I was in not having to face what Amelia was facing. I tried to emphasize to the ladies how blessed I was, but Amelia reached over, took my hand, and began to share with them about all the problems I had faced with my illness and consequent recovery from surgery.

I sat down beside Amelia, who was already wearing a hat. She opened my bag first and removed the special hat I had selected for her. Then she announced that she was going to try on each new hat as she opened it. She reached up to remove the hat she was already wearing and it was a terrifying moment for me. She had already lost so much of her hair that she had gone to her beautician to have her head shaved. There were large red sores on her scalp. I felt a sick feeling in the pit of my stomach, and had to work hard to remain calm and fight back tears. The reality of what she was facing and what I had been spared really hit me hard at that moment. I was so humbled that God, in His great mercy, had chosen to spare me from this dreadful disease.

I continued to be plagued with feelings of guilt. I remember the day I returned to Atlanta for one of my post-operative doctor appointments. I was sitting in the waiting area beside a kind middle-aged lady who learned I had just had surgery and was trying to prepare me for the long and difficult road ahead. She explained to me that I would have six chemotherapy treatments, and the oncologist would continue to follow me for five years, even if I did well and had no recurrence. I sat there and listened attentively. I just didn't have the heart to tell her my outcome had turned out so differently than hers. Why did God spare me and allow her to suffer like this? There are many questions like this that we ponder here. Many people say they have lots of questions for God when they get to heaven. I also have lots of unanswered questions. However, I have a feeling that when we get to heaven one day, those questions won't matter anymore.

I was intrigued that Amelia would have been drawn to me. I could sense that a special relationship was forming between us, and I found that rather interesting. Women who are unable to bear a child often have a difficult time being near a happy mother with her newborn baby. Those who have gone through the tragedy of divorce often find it difficult to continue socializing with a happily married couple. In a similar way, I was amazed that a woman who had just been diagnosed with ovarian cancer would choose to spend time with a woman who had miraculously been spared the same diagnosis. We both seemed to share this strong desire to spend time in fellowship together. God was truly at work. Several people commented they did not see how I could do this. Their comment was that they wouldn't know what to say or how to act around someone dealing with cancer. They thought getting involved would be too sad and emotional to handle. I shared with many people that I soon realized I was setting myself up for the biggest heartbreak I had ever faced, but I felt overwhelmly drawn toward this lady. She was always in my thoughts and prayers. I was constantly interceding for her healing. I was forever trying to think of something I could do to make this situation easier for her to bear. God had called me to minister to her, and I wasn't sure that I was capable of handling the job. However, I soon realized that my capability would not be as important as my availability.

He never calls us to a job without equipping us to handle it.

I looked forward to giving her a call or going up for a visit. I never had to worry about what to say, because we always had so much to talk about. Amelia shared with me one day about the difficult experience of losing her mother two years earlier. She felt that when her mother passed away she had lost her best friend and didn't know what she would do without her. Amelia related that when she met me, she felt that God gave her back so much of what she lost in her mother. She felt that God sent her the sister she never had. Amelia had begun keeping a journal of her feelings and experiences, and she wrote the following about our meeting that first day in Room 218 at the hospital: *"Patty told her friend about me and Patty had already told me about her. I had forgotten about her until I think it was the day I was going home from the hospital. I remember that I was well enough to be left alone for the first time and in to my room walks this nice looking lady wearing a very pretty sweater, and a very handsome man, neither of whom I had ever seen before. She introduces herself as Luanne Owensby and her husband, Bryan. She tells me that they are long time friends of Patty and that Luanne was back at the hospital to get her staples removed from surgery. She tells me that even though our oncologist had prepared them for a possible cancer diagnosis at surgery, it turned out-by the grace of God- to be severe endometriosis- not cancer. She told me they were praying for me and that she would be anxious to know how I was doing. Well, God has kept her by my side every minute since then- physically, emotionally, and spiritually. As I have shared with her- she and God have given back to me so much of what I lost when my mother died in 1999. They've given me back a sister, best friend, confidant- someone who knows all my warts and loves me in spite of them."* (Amelia's Journal)

I was somewhat amazed to find myself reaching out to this lady I had previously not known, and was also quite amazed that she was choosing to spend so much time with someone who had been spared the great difficulties she was now facing. However, I don't think either of us actually made the choice. I think we were chosen for each other by our Heavenly Father. Corrie Ten Boom once said, "Every experience God gives us, and every person that God puts in our life, is a preparation for the future that only He can see." This was all a part of His great plan for our lives, and it felt like a perfect plan. We were embarking on an incredible journey together. We were truly becoming sisters by divine appointment!

⊱Chapter Six⊰

HOPE FOR EACH DAY

I had returned to work at the end of April and found it to be more difficult than I had anticipated. Just after my surgery, new medical reports had been released concerning the danger of hormone replacement therapy and its link to breast and ovarian cancer. Additionally, my oncologist was concerned that this could cause a recurrence of the endometriosis that had been the source of my medical problems. He strongly encouraged me never to consider hormone replacement therapy. Interestingly, Amelia had no family history of cancer, and the oncologist was never able to determine the ideology of her cancer by studies that were conducted. However, Amelia had taken hormone replacement therapy for twenty years. She spoke to some women's groups during her illness and strongly encouraged them to avoid taking hormone replacement therapy. She felt very strongly that this was the origin of her problem. She related that she had a family history of early menopause and began experiencing symptoms of this by age forty. *"Unfortunately for me, this just happened to be occurring during the phase in medicine when there was a pill for everything! My physician prescribed a little pill for me, I popped it every day for twenty years and presumed that everything was fine. While I thought this little pill was curing me, it was actually killing me!" (Amelia's Journal).*

It was an easy decision for me to make, given the newly released medical information, my oncologist's recommendation, and Amelia's firsthand account of what she believed was the source of her cancer. My greatest adjustment to my very sudden and abrupt absence of hormones was the typical hot flashes, as well as severe insomnia. I would sometimes go several consecutive nights with hardly any sleep at all, and felt tired all the time. This had its good side and bad side. While I lay awake at night unable to sleep, I would pray and intercede for Amelia's healing. On the downside, I would return from work each day utterly exhausted. I would turn on my ceiling fan, lie down on my bed, and give Amelia a call. She had started her first of six chemotherapy treatments by this time. She was experiencing the typical side effects from the chemotherapy (Taxol and Carboplatin). She was very weak, was unable to eat because of sores in her mouth, and was experiencing neuropathy in her hands and feet. She had lost her hair but had opted not to get a wig. She was very hot natured and having no hair didn't seem to bother her at all. I was so touched that with all the difficulties she was going through, she told me on several occasions that she was praying daily for me and my problems with insomnia.

During the regular phone visits Amelia and I had, she briefly shared with me these difficulties she was experiencing secondary to the chemotherapy, and then she quickly moved on to the positives in her life. A positive attitude is always important, but particularly so when dealing with cancer. Her incredibly positive attitude was another reason I thought surely she would make it. Often when I asked how she was feeling, she said, "I'm all right," rather than giving me all the details of what wasn't going right. She often talked about other people she knew who were living with incurable illnesses and had no hope of ever being better. She continued to cling to the hope that these chemotherapy treatments were eventually going to be successful in resolving her problem. I continued to cling to that hope as well. *"But if we hope for what we do not see, we eagerly wait for it with perseverance" (Romans 8:25).* We did always look for the positive side of every negative situation she faced. We hoped that as the chemotherapy was destroying hair follicles and red blood cells, it was also destroying all the remaining cancer cells.

We were so encouraged and optimistic that our hope and perseverance were paying off. Every blood test revealed that the CA-125 level was declining. The CA-125 is a cancer tumor marker that is useful in the detection and treatment of ovarian cancer. Prior to Amelia's initial surgery, her CA-125 had been over 3000. The normal range is considered to be below 35. During this time of chemotherapy, not only was I calling often to check on her, but I also tried to send a card or letter to her each week to encourage her. After one particularly good report from blood tests, I sent this note:

May 23, 2002

Dear Amelia,

31.9! Wow! I can't tell you how excited I was to hear that! I even called Bryan in Florida just to tell him our good news. God is so good! His grace is so sufficient for our every need. Once again, I am reminded of Ephesians 3:20. He really is able to do "exceedingly abundantly above all that we ask or think, according to the power that works in us!" God has just outdone himself so many times in my prayer life in the past year. This verse became so real to me last fall on the weekend of September 11. I had planned to be at a women's retreat out of town that weekend, but after the September 11 attacks, I just wanted to stay at home with my family. Andrew, our son, had a football game that Friday night, and I became concerned that he might get injured and I wouldn't be there. (I was the parent with the medical background, and I just needed to be there in case of an injury!) I just about worried myself sick. I prayed and anguished over whether to go. I finally came to the realization that God had something special planned for me that weekend and Satan was trying to rob me of it. God finally gave me peace about going, and it was a wonderful weekend. I learned so much about God's grace, love, mercy, and forgiveness.

Anyway, I had prayed and prayed for God's protection to be on Andrew Friday night during the game. Late on Friday after-

noon, I learned that all high school football games in the state of Georgia had been cancelled that night because of the 9-11 attacks. I was so touched that God had known my concerns, heard my prayers, and answered them exceedingly and abundantly beyond what I had even asked or imagined!

One of the benefits of sharing in difficult times with our friends is that we also get to share in the joy that comes in the morning. 31.9 is one of those joys! I am so sorry that you continue to suffer with some of the related problems from your treatments. I'll just be praying specifically that those will continue to improve. Meanwhile, I hope they will seem to lessen in light of the good things that are happening to you. I just pray that this good report will be like a cool drink of water to a weary runner. May it refresh and renew your strength as you press on in this race! Remember, I'm still on the sidelines, cheering you on!

I love you and count it such a blessing to know you and share in this time with you,

Luanne

I had promised Amelia that I would come up for a visit when I finished work for the summer and she was feeling stronger. On June 11, 2002, I went to visit her at her home for the first time. I wanted to take a gift bag along, so I made a quick stop by a local bookstore. Not knowing Amelia very well, I didn't yet know her interests or hobbies, so I was really unsure what I should take to her. I knew she enjoyed reading, but didn't know how to choose a book she would enjoy or perhaps had not already read. My eyes drifted over to a little devotion book by Billy Graham entitled *Hope for Each Day*. I decided this would make a nice gift of encouragement for her so I dropped it into the little gift bag and was on my way. She kept this little book on the table beside the big recliner chair she used in her bedroom, and she read it daily. This book was returned to me on the day of her funeral service. Inside the front cover, she had written: Luanne-6/11/02. There was a handwritten prayer list folded inside that included the names of some people she was interceding for as well. The ribbon bookmark was placed on September 17, and the devotion talked about the sufficiency of God's grace. This was apparently the last day she had felt like reading from this little devotion book, but what a timely message she had read. She had been reminded that our sovereign God is still on His throne, and He is working out all things according to His plan. She had been reminded to keep her mind centered on Christ. *"You will keep him in perfect peace, Whose mind is stayed on You, Because he trusts in You..." (Isaiah 26:3).*

I had actually selected this book rather quickly on the day I had gone for my first visit with Amelia. It was only after the book was returned to me over two years later that I realized what an appropriate gift of encouragement it had been. In the preface of this book, Dr. Graham had expressed such an appropriate message for Amelia. He talked about the joy of walking with God each day, and knowing that the burdens of this life would soon pass, and we would be in the presence of God. He shared that we can have hope, because we can trust God's love to be with us in the bad times as well as in the good times.

It was Dwan Jacobsen Young who said, "The Lord wants us to be filled with hope- not just because it points us to a brighter tomorrow, but because it changes the quality of our lives." The Bible speaks often about hope. We find references to a blessed hope, a living hope, and the Lord Jesus Christ, our hope. I Peter 3:15 challenges us to *"always be ready to give a defense to everyone who asks you a reason for the hope that is in you, with meekness and fear."* Colossians 1:27 reminds us again of the source of our hope. It is *"Christ in you, the hope of glory."* Amelia had placed her hope and trust in Christ. *"Blessed is the man who trusts in the LORD, And whose hope is the LORD. For he shall be like a tree planted by the waters, Which spreads out its roots by the river, And will not fear when heat comes; But its leaf will be green, And will not be anxious in the year of drought, Nor will cease from yielding fruit" (Jeremiah 17:7-8).* Amelia's adversity had provided her the opportunity to find His faithfulness afresh. She was strengthened and encouraged as she meditated upon this faithfulness of God. Remembering His faithfulness gave her that unshakable hope she needed to press on in the midst of this adversity.

Scottish writer Samuel Smiles stated, "Hope is like the sun, which, as we journey toward it, casts the shadow of our burden behind us." She talked often of how she had experienced the love of God in such an overwhelming way during her illness. *"This was the first time I've ever felt so loved. If you've never been there, I simply don't have words to describe it!" (Amelia's Journal) "Therefore, having been justified by faith, we have peace with God through our Lord Jesus Christ, through whom also we have access by faith into this grace in which we stand, and rejoice in hope of the glory of God. And not only that, but we also glory in tribulations, knowing that tribulation produces perseverance; and perseverance, character; and character, hope. Now hope does not disappoint, because the love of God has been poured out in our hearts by the Holy Spirit who was given to us" (Romans 5:1-5).* Christ was indeed her hope of glory. Her faith had found a resting place. She was resting peacefully and confidently that her anchor in Christ would hold, in spite of the storm she was enduring. *"This hope we have as an anchor of the soul, both sure and steadfast..." (Hebrews 6:19).* She was standing assuredly on the solid rock. *"I will love You, O LORD, my strength. The LORD is my rock and my fortress and my deliverer; My God, my strength, in whom I will trust..." (Psalm 18:1-2).* Amelia's strong faith and positive attitude were a tremendous testimony to all who knew her. *"Now faith is the substance of things hoped for, the evidence of things not seen" (Hebrews 11:1).* Real faith is not just believing God can, but knowing that He will. Amelia had real faith and hope in Christ.

Hope is actually another of those intriguing words to me. Jean Kerr once said, "Hope is the feeling that the feeling you have isn't permanent." When we use the word *hope*, we typically mean that we anticipate or desire that something will happen. Those of us who have chosen to be followers of Christ don't have to hope in this context of the word. We have the assurance of the permanence of our salvation and the certainty of eternity with Christ. *"For this reason I also suffer these things; nevertheless I am not ashamed, for I know whom I have believed and am persuaded that He is able to keep what I have committed to Him until that Day" (II Timothy 1:12).* Amelia did not have to hope everything was going to be okay; she knew that she had the assurance that all was well with her soul.

Hope can give us a feeling of elevation during those low points in life. It gives us the anticipation and foresight that better days are ahead. Some doctors will acknowledge that their patient's hope is a very important element in the overall healing process. Recent studies have focused on the importance of hope and prayer for the recovery of the ill. Some medical schools are even beginning to incorporate a class into their curriculum on the connection of faith, hope, and healing. German poet Karl Ludwig von Knebel once stated, "Hope awakens courage. He who can implant courage in the human soul is the best physician."

Those of us who are in Christ also do not have to hope that we will spend eternity with Him. *"These things I have written to you who believe in the name of the Son of God, that you may know that you have eternal life, and that you may continue to believe in the name of the Son of God" (I John 5:13).* Amelia knew she had eternal life. She knew that God was at work in her life. She knew that the God who had given her salvation was transforming her into His likeness. She knew that God was in control and makes no mistakes. She knew that all of His promises are trustworthy. That is why she could be so calm in the midst of the storm. In Matthew 14:28-32, we have an account of Peter being caught in the midst of a storm. *"And Peter answered Him and said, "Lord, if it is You, command me to come to you on the water." So He said, "Come." And when Peter had come down out of the boat, he walked on the water to go to Jesus. But when he saw that the wind was boisterous, he was afraid; and beginning to sink he cried out, saying, "Lord, save me!" And immediately Jesus stretched out His hand and caught him, and said to him, "O you of little faith, why did you doubt?"* Peter was able to walk on water until he took his eyes off Jesus. He focused on his circumstances, and his faith became weak. When Peter looked down, Peter went down! Amelia was so strong in her faith, and she just never seemed to focus on her circumstances. She never complained or questioned why she was having to go through this storm. She had learned to submit to God, and be content in all circumstances. *"Not that I speak in regard to need, for I have learned in whatever state I am, to be content" (Philippians 4:11).* She kept her eyes on Christ and drew strength she needed to stand strong in the midst of her storm. It was Louisa Mae Alcott who said, "I am not afraid of the storm, for I am learning how to sail my own ship." Amelia was not afraid of this storm, for she had trusted Christ to sail her ship safely home. She was resting comfortably in the assurance of an eternal hope. *"If in this life only we have hope in Christ, we are of all men the most pitiable" (I Corinthians 15:19).* She lived her life daily with the assurance of Hebrews 13:5-6. *"Let your conduct be without covetousness; be content with such things as you have. For He Himself has said, "I will never leave you nor forsake you." So we may boldly say: "The Lord is my helper; I will not fear. What can man do to me?"* Amelia had no fear. She had experienced the perfect love of God, which drives out all fear (I John 4:18). God had taken away her fear, and placed a song of praise on her lips. *"I will bless the LORD at all times; His praise shall continually be in my mouth. My soul shall make its boast in the LORD; The humble shall hear of it and be glad. Oh, magnify the LORD with me, And let us exalt His name together. I sought the LORD, and He heard me, And delivered me from all my fears" (Psalm 34:1-4).* She had total peace and confidence that Christ would be with her, and all would be well. *"For I consider that the sufferings of this present time are not worthy to be compared with the glory which shall be revealed in us" (Romans 8:18).* Even in the midst of a diagnosis of terminal cancer, there is hope to be found. *"Remember the word to Your servant, Upon which You have caused me to hope. This is my comfort in my affliction, For Your word has given me life" (Psalm 119:49-50).* Hanging on

Amelia's bathroom wall, where she could daily read it, was an interesting and appropriate variation of the well known Serenity Prayer...

> God grant me the courage to change the things I can change.
> The serenity to accept those I cannot change.
> And the wisdom to know the difference.
> But God, grant me the courage not to give up
> on what I think is right
> Even though I think it is hopeless...

We all will face adverse situations in this life. After the storm strikes, it is too late to begin preparatory measures. What are we doing now that will better equip us for these times of difficulty? What is our anchor, and will it hold in spite of the storm? Will these inevitable situations make us bitter, or will they make us better? When we find ourselves in these difficult times, we need to know that we can always place our trust and hope in God. If Amelia could speak to those who are facing a storm and are experiencing discouragement today, I believe she would simply repeat the words of Psalm 43:5. "Why are you cast down, O my soul? And why are you disquieted within me? Hope in God..."

In every adversity, our source of hope, courage, and strength is Jesus Christ. *"Blessed be the God and Father of our Lord Jesus Christ, who according to His abundant mercy has begotten us again to a living hope..." (I Peter 1:3).* Amelia had the blessed assurance that she belonged to Christ. Christ alone was her living hope, and there was renewed hope in each new day that she faced. She had discovered that having faith, hope, and charity was truly the way to live successfully!

≻Chapter Seven≺

GRACE FOR EVERY NEED

One of the many lessons I learned from Amelia during our journey is that there really is sufficient grace for every need that we have. *"And God is able to make all grace abound toward you, that you, always having all sufficiency in all things, may have an abundance for every good work" (II Corinthians 9:8)*. While cancer is one of the ugliest words I know, grace is one of the most beautiful. Dan Roberts stated, "Grace is when God gives us what we don't deserve, and mercy is when God doesn't give us what we do deserve." Grace has been a difficult gift for me to understand. It has been said that if something seems too good to be true, it probably is! Grace would have to be an exception to that rule. Dwight L. Moody once said, "God never made a promise that was too good to be true." Grace does seem too good to be true, but God's grace is truth. God's grace is truly amazing. It is unmerited, divine favor of God. When I was just a child, I learned an easy to remember definition of grace from my dad. G-R-A-C-E is God's Riches At Christ's Expense. The motive of grace is the infinite love of our merciful Heavenly Father. It is a free gift from God, because Jesus paid the price. *"But the free gift is not like the offense. For if by the one man's offense many died, much more the grace of God and the gift by the grace of the one Man, Jesus Christ, abounded to many. And the gift is not like that which came through the one who sinned, For the judgment which came from one offense resulted in condemnation, but the free gift which came from many offenses resulted in justification. For if by the one man's offense death* reigned through the one, much more those who receive abundance of grace and of the gift of righteousness will reign in life through the One, Jesus Christ. Therefore, as through one man's offense judgment came to all men, resulting in condemnation, even so through one Man's righteous act the free gift came to all men, resulting in justification of life. For as by one man's disobedience many were made sinners, so also by one Man's obedience many will be made righteous. Moreover the law entered that the offense might abound. But where sin abounded, grace abounded much more, so that as sin reigned in death, even so grace might reign through righteousness to eternal life through Jesus Christ our Lord"* (Romans 5:15-21). God doesn't owe us anything, but He has given us everything. *"The young lions lack and suffer hunger; But those who seek the LORD shall not lack any good thing"* (Psalm 34:10). At Calvary, Jesus Christ did indeed pay a debt that He did not owe, because we owed a debt that we could never have paid. *"For you know the grace of our Lord Jesus Christ, that though He was rich, yet for your sakes He became poor, that you through His poverty might become rich"* (II Corinthians 8:9).

It was the gift of amazing grace that saved us, and that amazing grace also daily sustains us. *"But God, who is rich in mercy, because of His great love with which He loved us, even when we were dead in trespasses, made us alive together with Christ (by grace you have been saved), and raised us up together, and made us sit together in the heavenly places in Christ Jesus, that in the ages to come He might show the exceeding riches of His grace in His kindness toward us in Christ Jesus. For by grace you have been saved through faith, and that not of yourselves; it is the gift of God, not of works, lest anyone should boast. For we are His workmanship, created in Christ Jesus for good works, which God prepared beforehand that we should walk in them"* (Ephesians 2:4-10). Those of us who are in Christ do not become exempt from troubles and trials. In fact, some of the strongest believers in Christ have endured the most persecution, heartache, and difficulty. *"Yes, and all who desire to live godly in Christ Jesus will suffer persecution"* (II Timothy 3:12). While we are not exempt from suffering, we do have the promise that Christ will be with us during these difficult times. *"But now, thus says the LORD, who created you, O Jacob, And He who formed you, O Israel: "Fear not, for I have redeemed you; I have called you by your name; You are Mine. When you pass through the waters, I will be with you; And through the rivers, they shall not overflow you. When you walk through the fire, you shall not be burned, Nor shall the flame scorch you. For I am the LORD your God, The Holy one of Israel, your Savior"* (Isaiah 43:1-3). Christ uses these difficulties in our lives to strengthen us and draw us into a greater dependence on Him. His plan for us is always perfect. He always desires the very best for his children. *"For the LORD God is a sun and shield; The LORD will give grace and glory; No good thing will He withhold From those who walk uprightly"* (Psalm 84:11). It is during our times of weakness that Christ demonstrates His strength in our lives. His word affirms that His strength is made perfect during our times of weakness. His strength truly is perfect when our strength is gone.

Our God is omniscient and omnipotent, and He can actually cause unfortunate circumstances in our life to work for good to those of us who love Him. *"And we know that all things work together for good to those who love God, to those who are the called according to His purpose"* (Romans 8:28). Certainly all things that happen in our lives are not good, but all things can work together for good as we allow God to do His great work in us.

One day as Amelia and I were returning from a doctor's appointment in Atlanta, we were talking about how blessed our lives had been because of the times we had spent together and the experiences we had shared. I went on to say that I was sure she really wished she had never met me, because we probably would never have met if she had not been dealing with cancer. From that perspective, I would have to say that I also wish we had never met. However, the innumerable blessings that we each received through this difficult trial in her life, and the journey we shared, are examples of how God does make things work together for good in our lives if we love and trust Him.

We are often prone to forget our dependency and need for God in the good times of our lives. It is in the difficult times that we are more likely to recognize our desperate need for a Savior. *"I believed there was grace for every need, but I'd never had a need like this before." (Amelia's Journal)* We don't usually realize it, but on our very best day, we are still hopeless and helpless apart from God. We truly are totally dependent upon Him. I can't think of a more helpless situation than to be given a diagnosis of cancer. Yet I personally know several people who will verbalize that they are actually grateful they had cancer. *"...Therefore most gladly I will rather boast in my infirmities, that the power of Christ may rest upon me. Therefore I take pleasure in infirmities, in reproaches, in needs, in persecutions, in distresses, for Christ's sake. For when I am weak, then I am strong" (II Corinthians 12:9-10).* How could anyone express gratitude for a diagnosis of cancer? On the surface, we might be inclined to think this altered mentality must surely be another side effect of their chemotherapy! However, these people who are able to be grateful for their experience with battling cancer have come to realize that good things can come from a bad situation. God's word affirms that He can use harmful things to bring good into our lives. We may not be grateful for the situation, but we can be grateful in the situation. *"In everything give thanks; for this is the will of God in Christ Jesus for you" (I Thessalonians 5:18).*

While much progress has been made in the treatment of cancer in recent years, the prognosis still is often not good. This seems to be particularly true of ovarian cancer. It has been coined "the disease that whispers", or "the silent killer", because its symptoms are usually vague and it is often more advanced by the time of diagnosis. It was a difficult situation in her life, but God used so many people and so many circumstances to bring good into Amelia's life. She was one of those people who was amazed, often overwhelmed, by the blessings God sent her way during her battle with cancer. Amelia became able to receive this gift of grace from God, and allow it to strengthen and uplift her. *"I was buoyed up on the wings of prayer. That was the first time I've ever felt so loved. If you've never been there, I simply don't have words to describe the love I've felt." (Amelia's Journal)*

Amelia shared with me that she had always known that ultimately, in the very end, there was victory in Jesus for the believer. However, it was not until she succumbed to cancer that she learned there can be daily victory in Jesus in this life as well. In John 10:10, Jesus said, *"...I have come that they may have life, and that they may have it more abundantly."* Amelia learned so much about this incredibly abundant life during her illness. She learned that grace was God's solution for her every need. *"Let us therefore come boldly to the throne of grace, that we may obtain mercy and find grace to help in time of need" (Hebrews 4:16).*

Shortly after beginning her first round of six chemotherapy treatments, Amelia became very weak and also developed painful sores in her mouth. She was unable to prepare meals for herself, so ladies in her church brought in soups, gelatin, and other foods she could eat. I would always take a pound cake when I went up for a visit. She was amazed that people cared enough to prepare meals and bring them to her. Those meals were a gift of grace for a specific need she had at that time.

The telephone would usually ring several times during my visits with her. People who loved her and were concerned about her needs would call to see how things were going. They would ask if she needed anything, or if there was something they could do to help. There would often be a friend or neighbor that dropped by to check on her when I was there. I was also there on more than one occasion when Kim and the boys would drop in for their visit after school. They always brought in her mail, and there would be letters and cards of encouragement daily that people had taken the time to send. Those cards and letters meant so much to her as she read them over and over again. The telephone calls, visits, cards, and letters were all gifts of grace for the present need.

Amelia never had to worry about traveling in to Atlanta alone for those often dreaded chemotherapy treatments. Someone always volunteered to take her. She sometimes had more than one volunteer for the same day. She was overwhelmed that people were concerned enough about her to give their time to transport her on this hour long trip into Atlanta. Those volunteer drivers were a gift of grace for a specific need that Amelia had.

Some of us sat lovingly and attentively by her side, holding her hand and encouraging her during those long hours of chemotherapy treatments. Sometimes we went for a warm blanket and tucked it around her as she settled in for the duration of the treatment. Sometimes we pushed the I. V. pole and helped her into the restroom. Sometimes we walked across the street and brought her back a snack from Chick-fil-A. At other times we just sat quietly by her side and offered up prayers of intercession for her strength and healing while she took a short nap. All of these acts of love and kindness were simply gifts of grace during her time of need.

There was always someone available to go with her to a doctor's appointment. She would sometimes verbalize that she would be fine to go alone, but she would always breathe a sigh of relief when I told her I'd meet her at Wal Mart in Villa Rica and go with her. She often got bad news on these visits, but she never had to hear it alone. Someone was there to hold her hand and offer love, support, and encouragement. I was often the blessed person who had the privilege of going with Amelia to her doctor's appointment. It was always good to see the doctor and nurses who had taken care of me in my time of need. I would remind them that they had done such a good job in caring for me, and I expected them to do the same for her. We also discovered that two sets of ears were better able to hear and retain all the important information that was given during each doctor visit. Those of us who were able to give of ourselves and our time were constantly reminded that it is indeed more blessed to give than to receive. We were also reminded of the value of being a friend, and having a friend. *"Two are better than one, Because they have a good reward for their labor. For if they fall, one will lift up his companion. But woe to him who is alone when he falls, For he has no one to help him up"* *(Ecclesiastes 4:9-10).*

Amelia usually didn't mind going in for her scheduled appointments. We would say, "We'll celebrate if it's good news, and we'll just be glad they found it and can do something about it if it's bad news." When we got good news, she always felt so much better, so relieved and encouraged to press on. Unfortunately, we rarely got good news. I suppose the most memorable visit was in February of 2004. It was the day she was diagnosed with the last recurrence. We knew things were not going well. She was again retaining fluid in the abdomen and her CA-125 level was continuing to rise. Our oncologist came into the treatment room, and after examining her, he related that the pelvic exam that day was actually good. Then he opened her chart and was calm but matter of fact as he shared with us that the cancer was back. It was so hard for us to hear, but not a surprise. This time there were masses on the liver and pancreas, as well as a splattering across the abdomen. There would be no more surgery, but it would be necessary to begin a new chemotherapy regime. After he left the room, tears began to trickle down her face. This was the first time I had seen her cry throughout this entire long and difficult ordeal. She was growing tired and weary in the battle. I stepped over to the edge of the treatment table where she sat, and embraced her tightly for a long while as we wept together. Neither of us uttered a word, but both of us feared we might be fighting a losing battle. It was a devastating blow. Other than the initial short eleven months after the first round of chemotherapy treatments, the past two years had been spent going through surgery, chemotherapy, more surgery, and more chemotherapy.

I was actually not surprised that she quickly regained her composure and started looking for the positives in the situation. She expressed joy and gladness that the new masses were small, and there was another chemotherapy drug available to try. She dried her tears, and we left the treatment room. She met her doctor in the hallway, gave him a big hug, looked him in the eyes, and said, "Don't you worry about me. I'm going to be all right!" *"Watch, stand fast in the faith, be brave, be strong" (I Corinthians 16:13).*

Her most immediate concerns that afternoon were telling Kim the bad news, and wondering if she could get through the remainder of the school year while taking these new chemotherapy treatments. She had a passion for teaching school children and felt so bad that the last two school years had been interrupted by surgeries and treatments. She never wanted to worry Kim and sometimes chose not to tell her the whole story after these doctor visits. She was always concerned that Kim was so busy with work and raising a family, and she didn't want to be a burden to her. God's grace was so incredibly sufficient for Amelia that she sometimes didn't even appear to grasp the severity of the situation we were facing. She would verbalize that she felt as though Kim was stressed and worried about something, and she just didn't know what was bothering her. She would name over various things she thought could be the culprit. I found it most interesting that she never included her illness in that list. I never had the heart to point that out to her.

We left the doctor's office and arrived back at the car. I suggested that we should just say a prayer for sufficient strength and grace for our present needs before we headed back home. I was planning to pray, but my attempt only yielded a quivering voice that was too devastated at the moment to audibly express the needs and desires of my heart. Amelia, with all her unwavering courage and strength, reached over and grasped my hand. "Let me pray," she said. And indeed she did pray the most courageous prayer I have ever heard, with total composure, confidence, and peace. How could she do that? *"He gives power to the weak, And to those who have no might He increases strength. Even the youths shall faint and be weary, And the young men shall utterly fall, But those who wait on the LORD Shall renew their strength; They shall mount up with wings like eagles, They shall run and not be weary, They shall walk and not faint" (Isaiah 40:29-31).* In the midst of her weakness and suffering, Christ was truly renewing her strength. *"But may the God of all grace, who called us to His eternal glory by Christ Jesus, after you have suffered a while, perfect, establish, strengthen, and settle you" (I Peter 5:10).*

I was given a note card and magnet several years ago that made its way to my refrigerator door and remains there today. It says: "God is good... God is love, and He cannot go against His own nature. When pain and hurt, cancer, and even 9-11's happen, He is not the source of them. He is the grace that guides us through." Amelia's life reinforced the truth in the words of the old hymn penned by John Newton over two hundred years ago about God's *Amazing Grace:*

Amazing grace! How sweet the sound that
saved a wretch like me!
I once was lost but now am found; Was blind, but now I see.
'Twas grace that taught my heart to fear,
And grace my fears relieved.
How precious did that grace appear the hour I first believed!
Thro' many dangers, toils, and snares I have already come.
"Tis grace hath bro't me safe thus far,
And grace will lead me home.
When we've been there ten thousand years,
Bright shining as the sun,
We've no less days to sing God's praise
than when we'd first begun.

It truly was grace that had brought her safe thus far. It was that same grace that would ultimately lead her home. *"But by the grace of God I am what I am, and His grace toward me was not in vain; but I labored more abundantly than they all, yet not I but the grace of God which was with me" (I Corinthians 15:10).* I never ceased to be amazed at the strength, courage, peace, and calmness she constantly demonstrated in the midst of one storm after another. There could only be one possible explanation for how she was able to consistently do this. *"And the grace of our Lord was exceedingly abundant, with faith and love which are in Christ Jesus" (I Timothy 1:14).* There truly was grace for every need!

≻Chapter Eight≺

AMELIA'S ANGELS

I believe there are angels all around us. Sometimes we have trouble seeing them because we are looking for wings. Sometimes we don't recognize them because we are looking with physical, rather than spiritual eyes. These celestial beings have been quite intriguing, and the topic of much study and conversation. Many books have been written about angelic encounters. Angels are mentioned more than two hundred times in thirty- five books of the Bible. They were created by God to serve Him and minister to others. *"But when He again brings the firstborn into the world, He says: "Let all the angels of God worship Him." And of the angels He says: "Who makes His angels spirits And His ministers a flame of fire"* *(Hebrews 1:6-7).* God has assigned some of these angelic beings the role of praising Him. In Isaiah 6:1-3, we find a group of seraphim engaged in worship. *"In the year that King Uzziah died, I saw the Lord sitting on a throne, high and lifted up, and the train of His robe filled the temple. Above it stood seraphim; each one had six wings; with two he covered his face, with two he covered his feet, and with two he flew. And one cried to another and said: "Holy, holy, holy is the Lord of hosts; The whole earth is full of His glory!"* Angels have again become a popular subject of art in recent years. Movies and television shows have been based on these guardian spirits. Angels have often been used as messengers from God. They guide, instruct, and protect God's people. In the first chapter of Luke, we are given the account of the angel Gabriel who was sent by God to announce

56

to Mary that she had found favor with God. *"Then the angel said to her, "Do not be afraid, Mary, for you have found favor with God. And behold, you will conceive in your womb and bring forth a Son, and shall Call His name Jesus" (Luke 1:30-31).*

Many people believe they have a guardian angel. Psalm 91:11-12 reminds us that every child of God is under the watchful eye of the angelic host. *"For He shall give His angels charge over you, To keep you in all Your ways. In their hands they shall bear you up, Lest you dash your foot against a stone."* An old hymn entitled *Angels Watching Over Me* suggests that we have multiple angels watching over us at all times.

Some people are described as angels because of their acts of love and kindness. Hebrews 1:14 states, *"Are they not all ministering spirits, sent forth to minister for those who will inherit salvation?"* I have read with interest of incidences in which people were in a crisis situation and believe an angelic encounter spared their life. *"The angel of the Lord encamps all around those who fear Him, And delivers them" (Psalm 34:7).* In most of these instances, the person relates that after the crisis situation was resolved, the angel was nowhere to be found. *"Do not forget to entertain strangers: for by so doing some have unwittingly entertained angels" (Hebrews 13:2).* I have actually known several people personally who believe they have experienced this kind of invisible intervention.

In the late 1970's, a television show called *Charlie's Angels* became very popular. As I remember, Charlie was an anonymous detective who gave assignments to three ladies to assist him in solving crimes. These three ladies were considered Charlie's angels, and they were always busy working to accomplish the mission they had been assigned.

Amelia also believed in angels. She believed that God brought a host of people into her life to be her angels, and to assist her in accomplishing the mission God had chosen for her. She called these people her angels. It has been said that friends are quiet angels who lift us to our feet when our wings have trouble remembering how to fly. We can look back now and see that God was indeed planting people in Amelia's path that would be there to assist and encourage her during her time of adversity. *"Behold, I send an Angel before you, to keep you in the way, and to bring you into the place which I have prepared" (Exodus 23:20).* Amelia had written about many of her angels in her journal...

"B. C.- Before cancer I'd never really considered angels. But now I see them everywhere!" (Amelia's Journal)

"Through the Holy Spirit, God sends me circumstances and people (I call them my angels), to minister to me and guide me home." (Amelia's Journal)

Amelia was an elementary school teacher, and she considered her school principal to be one of her angels. *"I believe that he is another one of my angels that God has sent to me to show me the way home." (Amelia's Journal)*

"I was going through my first six rounds of chemotherapy when I finally joined a Sunday School class, and attendance is still not where I want it to be, because of another surgery and recovery from the last six chemo treatments. That has not slowed the love, prayers, and support of my angels that are in my church family. They lift me up night and day to the Lord." (Amelia's Journal)

"I'm always at a loss for words when I try to express what my school means to me. God had that support group set up for a long time. He knew how I would come to need the special things that only they could give. The love and caring that we share is often too emotional for us to talk about. Their love, the cards, letters, calls, concern- the support they give me at school and at all times never stops. I am lifted continually on the wings of their prayers." (Amelia's Journal)

"What can I say- God, my precious daughter Kim, and Luanne hold my hand night and day along side all the other angels God has blessed me with. All my angels at work have been known to do the same thing at times. Just in different places. (Amelia's Journal)

"All the churches who have prayed for me-Praise God for your faithfulness. You are my angels, too. You've helped me to

stand- when without you and God, I would have fallen in hope-lessness. I thank and praise God for you all!" (Amelia's Journal)

"Surgery, April 10th- All my prayer warriors are at work-Here- There- Everywhere. Many of my angels are with me." (Amelia's Journal)

"Ann, Ken's mom, has been and continues to be a special angel to me and many others." (Amelia's Journal)

"My Sunday School teacher and his wife, also fellow choir members, sweet, sweet spirits. Donna is with me again- as always. I was especially thankful to have our minister there. We all held hands and had prayer and fellowship. With the help of all my prayer warriors and angels, I was lifted up to the mountain-top!" (Amelia's Journal)

I believe God sent many angels, both visible and invisible, to minister to Amelia during her two and a half year journey with cancer. During her last hospitalization, I went up for a visit. She had been admitted for a few days to try to recharge her engine, as she described it. She was very weak because she had been unable to eat for several weeks. She was having difficulty breathing because she was retaining large amounts of fluid. During this hospitalization, four liters of fluid were withdrawn from her abdomen, and she was given intravenous feedings to strengthen her. This visit proved to be another painful reality check for me. Amelia had always been on the second floor, the obstetrics and gynecology floor. When I arrived at the hospital, I realized that she had been admitted to a different floor. My investigation of this revealed what I had fearfully suspected. This time, she had been placed on the oncology floor. As always, something good comes in the midst of a bad situation. This particular day, the good came in the form of a special little nurse. This young lady came in and out of the room several times that day while I was at Amelia's bedside. She was very kind and friendly, and I sensed a special, sweet spirit within her. After I left that evening, she came into the room and asked Amelia if I was her sister. This gave Amelia the perfect opportunity to share our God story about being sisters by divine appointment. Then the nurse began to

share her God story. A church had taken her family in and ministered to them when they moved to America from an Asian
country. They had supported her family materially, emotionally,
and spiritually as they established their new home in America.
Her mom had worked so hard to ensure that each of her six children received a good education. This little nurse had wanted so
badly to become a missionary, but had ultimately entered nursing
school. It was a quiet night on the oncology floor, and she spent
some extra time with Amelia that evening, sharing with her about
the goodness of the Lord in her life. It was another time Amelia
had felt a special communion with God and the angel He had sent
her way. I have often wished I could go back to the hospital and
find that sweet little nurse. I'd like to tell her that her dream had
come true. She really had become a missionary!

I had felt a clear call from God on that Wednesday night as I
sat alone in my study and typed the note I would leave with
Amelia on my first visit to the hospital when I met her. God had
called me to encourage and minister to Amelia. She had often
introduced me as her angel. Early in our friendship, I learned a
great deal about intercessory prayer, as I was continually lifting
Amelia up before the Lord, and praying for healing, strength,
peace, and contentment for her. I had continued to be plagued by
insomnia after my surgery, but that was another situation in
which something good had come from something bad. I could literally pray around the clock for Amelia's needs.

One day while strolling through a Christian bookstore, my
eyes wandered to a shelf of beautiful Willow Tree angels. I was
particularly drawn to the Angel of Prayer, and on the back of the
card it read: Prayer- Bless and keep all safe. I decided this would
make a special gift for Amelia. She took this little angel to school
and sat it on her desk to remind her that one of her angels was
ever interceding for her. This angel was returned to me after
Amelia's passing. On the bottom of it she had written: Luanne-
9/20/02. It now sits in a special place in the foyer of my home.

I have another very special angel that sits on a shelf in my
family room. This golden angel of cut glass and metal stands tall

and stately. She holds a songbook in her hands and is illuminated by a small votive candle. This is the angel that Amelia brought to me on the first Christmas we shared together in 2002. It was too beautiful and meaningful to pack away after the holidays, so it remains nearby throughout the year. It reminds me that my special angel, Amelia, now watches over me.

➤Chapter Nine◄

THE LITTLE OLD RUGGED CROSS

Amelia had an incredibly positive attitude in the midst of this difficult storm in her life. One might suspect that she had previously had a great life, free of the typical problems and difficulties we all face. Amelia verbalized that her life had been a great one. In reality, Amelia had faced much heartache and disappointment. Some of her greatest hopes and dreams for her life had been shattered. In the early 1980's, she had to come to grips with the fact that her marriage was in trouble. She was devastated and did everything she knew to do in her attempt to hold it together. Sadly, it was not meant to be.

This became a very dark and difficult time in Amelia's life. She searched many different avenues for solutions to her crisis. She tried to solve her problems on her own, but realized she did not have the answers. She turned on her television one day during this period of time, and Dr. Robert Schueller was delivering one of his messages on the power of positive thinking from the Crystal Cathedral in California. He caught her attention and ministered to her need that day. Consequently, she mailed a monetary gift to Dr. Schueller's program and soon received a response back. Included in the return letter from the Crystal Cathedral was a small gift, a little metal cross. There was nothing fancy about this little cross. It had a rough, pewter colored finish. It was approximately one inch tall and was attached to a key ring.

However, there was something special about this cross. It is through the cross that God made Himself totally available to us. The cross reminds us of the hope, joy, love, peace, strength, and trust that we have in Christ alone. Amelia began to put the little cross in her pocket each morning as she dressed for work. She kept it with her at all times and shared with me how important it was to her to have it with her when she was going through the entire difficult process of her divorce. When she was overcome with anxiety, thoughts of hurt, anger, frustration, sadness, or disappointment, she would slip her hand into her pocket and cling to the little cross.

During this time in her life, Amelia was not actively involved in a church. She found it difficult to go alone to many of the places that had previously been an important part of her life. Her extent of praise and worship was largely a prayer that she proudly repeated daily. *"As background, you need to know that for 17 years prior to 2000, I had prayed this same prayer everyday: "Lord, I offer myself to Thee, to build with me and do with me as Thy wilt. Remove the bondage of self that I might better be able to do Thy will. Take away my difficulties that the victory over them might bear witness to those I would help- of Thy love, Thy power, and Thy way of life." Humbling prayer, isn't it? I loved saying this prayer for 17 years and still it gives me goose-bumps even though it took me an hour to recall it exactly for today. I don't use it anymore. The prayers by rote have gone. I pray that this is a good sign from God, a closer relationship with Him."* (Amelia's Journal)

It was during this time, when Amelia initially received the cross, that a good friend was diagnosed with breast cancer. Amelia remembered another interesting coincidence as she shared with me the story of this friend's illness. She had her surgery at the same hospital and had been placed in Room 218, the room Amelia and I had shared years later. *"Luanne left the hospital room that I got. When she and her husband came to visit me, I remembered that this was the same room that my dearest friend was in when she had breast cancer. Ain't God amazing!*

He's getting me to listen now." (Amelia's Journal) Amelia had gone to visit this friend shortly after her surgery for cancer. She told her the story about hearing the message on the importance of positive thinking and being given the little cross. As her visit ended that day, Amelia decided to leave the cross with this special friend. It was Amelia's hope and prayer that the little cross would also remind her of this higher power that could provide strength and encouragement during the storm she was facing, as it had done for Amelia during some very difficult days.

Over the years, Amelia had lost contact with this friend, who had moved away. She had forgotten about the cross she had given her almost twenty years earlier. However, in the summer of 2003, this dear friend was passing through Villa Rica on her way to a vacation at the beach. She had heard of Amelia's illness and made plans to stop by for a visit. On that day, she returned the little metal cross to Amelia, and the pattern resumed. Each morning as Amelia dressed and prepared for the day, she would slip the little cross into her pocket. She reached into her pocket often throughout the day, clinging to the cross and being reminded that her strength and help did indeed come from the Lord. One of Amelia's favorite scriptures became Psalm 121, and was read at her funeral service. *"I will lift up my eyes to the hills- From whence comes my help? My help comes from the Lord, Who made heaven and earth. He will not allow your foot to be moved; He who keeps you will not slumber. Behold, He who keeps Israel Shall neither slumber nor sleep. The Lord is your keeper; The Lord is your shade at your right hand. The sun shall not strike you by day, Nor the moon by night. The Lord shall preserve you from all evil; He shall preserve your soul. The Lord shall preserve your going out and your coming in From this time forth, and even forevermore."*

The cross is the proof of God's love for us. Amelia's total confidence rested in the cross. I recall sitting by Amelia's side several times during long hours of chemotherapy treatments. She would cling to my hand on one side, and cling to the little cross nestled in her pocket with her other hand. It was comforting to her to have a friend and a cross to cling to during this time of uncertainty. She found strength, courage, peace, and hope in this routine. Once after I had taken her for a chemotherapy treatment, she called and was obviously disturbed. She had slipped her hand into her pocket that evening and the cross was missing. She had called the infusion center, and they had not been able to find it there. I went out to my car, and thankfully, the little cross was wedged safe and secure into the back of the seat.

Shortly before we were leaving for the mission trip to Europe, I was experiencing some anxiety regarding my daughter's surgery and impending pathology reports. Amelia reached into her pocket and pulled out the little cross. She wanted me to take it with me on the trip. I was very reluctant to do so, fearing that I might lose it somewhere along the way. Amelia insisted that I take it, reassuring me that if I lost the cross in Europe, it would be because it was supposed to be taken and left there.

During the last few weeks of her illness, Amelia was no longer able to dress in street clothes during the day. She had no pocket for the cross, so she had apparently put it away. I had not thought about it until I went to visit on Monday of the last week before her passing. Amelia seemed agitated that day, and it bothered me to see her that way. I mentioned to Kim later that evening that if we let her hold the special little cross, this very familiar object might be calming and reassuring to her. Unfortunately, we did not know where she had put the cross.

On the Sunday morning of Amelia's funeral service, Kim had searched again unsuccessfully for the cross. I did not know until after the service that day that Kim had hoped to find the cross that morning so that she could give it to me before the service. I could certainly have used it, because that was definitely one of those days when I needed a reminder that our help and strength are found in the cross.

After the service, we went back to Amelia's house, and it was then that Kim told me she had searched for the cross but had been unable to find it. She related that they did find a small, worn, rugged looking little cross, but she knew this surely was not the special cross she had heard about. I asked to see this cross she had found, and it was indeed the one! I was so touched that Kim would choose such a special gift to give to me as a remembrance of my dear friend and our precious journey together with this little cross. Although I would never have asked for it, that would have definitely been my choice of a personal item to keep as a remembrance of Amelia. I keep this cross with me every day, and often reach for, and cling to, this old rugged cross.

One day I noticed that a telephone number was etched into the back of this little cross. Curiosity got the best of me and I decided to dial this number. When I did, I heard the following message: "You have reached the counseling center of the Crystal Cathedral." I wondered how many other people may have received strength and encouragement from this organization over the past twenty years. I wondered how many other people might have a small, pewter colored cross that they have clung to for the past twenty years. It was an encouragement to me to know they continue to offer this service to people who need strength, hope, comfort, and encouragement.

Amelia did indeed cling to the old rugged cross, both physically and spiritually. In the early hours of Saturday morning, October 9, 2004, she exchanged the old cross for a crown. *"Blessed is the man who endures temptation; for when he has been approved, he will receive the crown of life which the Lord has promised to those who love Him" (James 1:12).* I am so honored that Kim chose to pass this special little old rugged cross on to me. I'll cherish it and carry on Amelia's pattern of clinging to it in times of need, until the day I exchange my cross for a crown.

⊁Chapter Ten⊰

AMELIA

I've always had an interest in names and their meaning. I remember when we were expecting our first child. My mother was growing increasingly more concerned as we were two weeks from our delivery date and had still not decided on a name for the baby. My husband and I felt this was one of those major decisions we would make for our child that would have lifelong implications. Not only were we interested in choosing a name that we liked the sound of, but we were also interested in the meaning of the name. We bought several of those books on baby names, and spent hours going through them. Many people don't really like the name that was chosen for them. As a child, I remember being with friends and discussing what we would change our name to if we had the opportunity to do so.

Amelia loved her name. She mentioned this on more than one occasion when we were together. I found that statement interesting as I remembered childhood conversations about changing the name you had been given. As I thought more about her statement, I became curious about the meaning of the name Amelia. I pulled out some of those old baby name books and dusted them off. I wasn't at all surprised with what I found. Amelia means "ambitious, industrious, hardworking, beloved, work of the Lord."

There were some other descriptive words I had expected to find that were not there. I had thought I might find the word *adventurous*. Amelia shared many stories of her adventures with me. I suppose one of my favorites was about her train trip to

Alabama. Amelia's boyfriend was several years older, and he had already gone away to college. He had wanted her to come down for his homecoming dance, and she thought that sounded like it would be lots of fun. Her parents had decided that was not a good idea. Not to be defeated, Amelia devised a plan to get to Auburn. She arranged to spend the weekend with a cousin, packed her bags, and was out of the house. However, she didn't go to her cousin's house. She went to the train station in Villa Rica, and was on her way to Alabama. Her parents became suspicious, found out she wasn't at her cousin's house, and they were soon on their way to Alabama as well. She hadn't been there long when they arrived, and her adventure was over. It was a long, quiet ride back to Villa Rica.

I also thought I might have found the word *organizer* used to describe Amelia. One of Amelia's sayings was, "There's a place for everything, and everything has a place." This was very true at her house. Everything was in its place, and she had no excess stuff lying around that she did not need or use. Her closets were neatly organized. I recall one day when I was visiting with her and did her laundry. When everything was folded and ready to put away, she sent me to the other side of the house to store linens in a closet there. When I opened the door, she had linens all neatly placed in their respective stack with labels on the shelves below each stack which read: full size fitted sheets, queen size flat sheets, etc. I was very careful to place everything in the proper place! She loved for her grandsons to come down to her house, but there were rules to be followed. They had a specific place to store their shoes while they were there. That way, no time would be lost hunting shoes when it was time to leave. As her illness progressed, she was taking quite a bit of medication each day. She had devised a system for this and took her pills in a specific order. We would stand by and patiently wait for her to swallow each one in their respective order. She had also very meticulously filed away a copy of all her medical records during this time. When we were packing away her belongings, we found her four drawer file cabinet to be filled with all her insurance forms, explanation of benefits, lab reports, X-ray reports, and pathology reports from her surgeries. It was probably more precise than her file at the oncology office.

This characteristic actually proved quite helpful during those last few weeks when Amelia became too weak to be ambulatory and had to send her caregivers to find what she needed. It was not a problem, because she knew exactly where to send us for whatever she needed. She was always very specific in her instructions. During those last couple of weeks, she often would ask for ice chips. She would measure with her fingers to show us how much to bring. Holding her fingers about an inch apart, she would say, "Bring me this much." We would go into the kitchen, get her little manual ice crusher, and be sure to bring back just one inch of crushed ice! The only time I found myself on a scavenger hunt was the last night I stayed with her. She had not rested at all that night, and I had been sent for one inch of crushed ice several times. Then she decided she wanted to hold a corn chip in her mouth to taste the salt. She told me to look outside her bedroom door on the coat rack for the bag of corn chips. Knowing those organizational skills she possessed, I did not question this unusual instruction. I didn't find them there, so she sent me to look in her closet. I didn't find them there either. I should have known to look in the kitchen for corn chips, but I just knew that Amelia had a place for everything, and she always knew where that place was. I did eventually find the corn chips in the kitchen!

Our Amelia was indeed ambitious, industrious, and hardworking. After high school, she got married and entered Auburn University. Kim was born before Amelia had completed her educational plans. However, her mother encouraged her to return to school and finish her degree. She was so grateful to her mother for helping her to accomplish this. It wasn't easy to return to school with household duties and a baby. Because Amelia was ambitious and a hard worker, she did return to West Georgia College, and completed her degree in Elementary Education. This college degree became especially important after her divorce, when she became a single parent and needed to provide for herself and Kim.

Amelia worked hard at being a good family member. I enjoyed many stories she shared about her family. Amelia didn't have a large family. She was an only child to her parents, and Kim was her only child. She loved to tell of experiences she and her mother had shared in the past. She loved her mother so much, and still would become emotional when speaking of her illness and death in 1999.

Amelia loved Kim and her family, and considered them to be her pride and joy. Amelia had regrets about Kim's childhood because of the family difficulties she went through during this time. She felt that she had failed Kim in many ways, but was so pleased with the fine young lady Kim had become. She paid Kim the highest of compliments in her journal. *"Many are the times that I have thought- when I grow up, I'd like to be just like my Kim- That's the greatest compliment I can think of. I've never felt that way about anyone else. Never wanted to be a movie star or President. She gets all my respect."* (Amelia's Journal) Amelia was always concerned about Kim's busy schedule, but admired her so much for being such a good mother to her boys, and a hard worker at her job. Amelia tried so hard to protect Kim from some of the difficulties she was facing. She didn't want to impose on her, knowing she had a busy schedule with a full-time job and family responsibilities. She sometimes chose not to tell Kim all the details from a bad doctor visit. I was with her on more than one occasion when she would get bad news. On the way home she would say, "I'm just not going to tell Kim right now. I don't want to worry her."

Not only did Amelia love and appreciate Kim, Ken, Adam, and Tyler, they loved her as well, and showed it by their actions. Long before her illness, they had been instrumental in getting Amelia back into church. She was ever so grateful for their encouragement to do that. During her illness, Kim and Ken ran errands for her and did things for her around the house that she was unable to do. During my first visit to Amelia's house, Kim called while I was there. She was picking up groceries for Amelia and made a thoughtful telephone call just to ask, "What flavor of Gatorade do you want?" Living next door, they made their afternoon stop to check in on Amelia. She looked forward to those visits as they dropped off her mail and visited with her. They always greeted her with a hug and kiss. Tyler was still small enough to sit in her lap, and she loved spending this special time with them and hearing about their day at school. There was usually a large jigsaw puzzle on the card table that Amelia and the boys would work on when they came to Nana's house. Amelia loved her family and they obviously loved her.

Amelia also worked hard at being a good teacher. She loved her job and the people with whom she worked. Her co-workers were on her angel list. She wanted to carry her load, and didn't expect any special favors during her illness. She expressed regret that her last two school years had been interrupted by her illness, surgeries, and chemotherapy treatments. She had tried to work her medical appointments around her work schedule as much as she could. Sadly, she had hoped to be able to teach for several more years.

Amelia worked hard at being a good friend. Several friends shared stories with me during her illness about acts of friendship and kindness she had shown to them. One friend shared about family vacations they spent together, and about playing golf with Amelia. Apparently Amelia also worked hard at being a good golfer. I was told she played well and took her golf game very seriously. Amelia worked hard at being a good friend to me. Our friendship started with my call to be a friend and encourager to her, but she became a dear friend and encourager to me. She taught me so much about life. She was a good listener, a good decision maker, and I respected and appreciated her advice. She taught me that while it is more blessed to give than to receive (Acts 20:35), it is also impossible to give without receiving. She taught me a lot about living, and a lot about dying.

I only had the opportunity to know Amelia for two and one-half short years. The things I know about most of her life are stories that were shared with me. During the period of time I knew her, the area in which I saw her as most industrious and hardworking was in her Christian faith and walk with God. We can know how strong a tree is by how well it weathers the storm.

Jesus said, *"I am the true vine, and My Father is the vine-dresser. Every branch in Me that does not bear fruit He takes away; and every branch that bears fruit He prunes, that it may bear more fruit"* (John 15:1-2). God had begun a pruning process in 2000 as she got back into church. She became actively involved in service and began to grow in her faith and relationship with Christ. God was preparing her for the storm she would face. Chances are that before this time, she might not have weathered the storm as well. As a result of the pruning process in her life, and the growth that was occurring as a result, she began to bear more fruit.

Amelia worked hard at living out Galatians 5:22-23. *"But the fruit of the Spirit is love, joy, peace, longsuffering, kindness, goodness, faithfulness, gentleness, self-control."* This scripture was very important to her, and she shared it when speaking to church groups about her experience with cancer. Her pastor had also noted her ability to continue bearing much fruit throughout her difficult battle with cancer, and he shared this same scripture at her funeral service. It is God's desire that we develop fruit of the spirit, so that we not only live a fulfilled life, but also so that others will see and desire these qualities. Matthew 7:20 reminds us that we are known by our fruit. It may not be so difficult to bear good fruit when everything is going our way, but the real test comes when we go through the storm. Amelia passed the fruit inspection!

Amelia knew of the amazing *LOVE* of God. She had experienced the Love of God in her life, and she demonstrated love to others. She was an affectionate person who could say so much without uttering a word. The first day I met her at the hospital, she immediately reached over the bed rail and grasped my hand. She held on tightly until it was time for me to go. She understood the importance of the human touch, and she knew how to really give a hug. She found it easy to say, "I love you," and you knew that she really meant it. 1Corinthians 13 describes the characteristics of this kind of love. *"Love suffers long and is kind; love does not envy; love does not parade itself, is not puffed up; does not behave rudely, does not seek its own, is not provoked, thinks no evil; does not rejoice in iniquity, but rejoices in the truth; bears all things, believes all things, hopes all things, endures all things. Love never fails."* Amelia had reason to demand attention, but she continued to verbalize, "It's not about me!" She continued to minister to others in love during the course of her own illness. She had an elderly aunt who lived nearby, and she frequently stopped in to check on her and help with her needs. During the last year of Amelia's life, she barely had energy to look after herself, yet she worried about her aunt's needs. She took her for an optometrist visit, to doctors' appointments, and helped make important long-term arrangements so that she could be assured her needs would be met. *"Be kindly affectionate to one another with brotherly love, in honor giving preference to one another; not lagging in diligence, fervent in spirit, serving the Lord; rejoicing in hope, patient in tribulation, continuing steadfastly in prayer; distributing to the needs of the saints, given to hospitality"* *(Romans 12:10-13).* Even though her physical health and strength were fading, she remained strong and courageous in the Lord. She recognized the source of her strength. The measureless love of God endures the test of time. Amelia had discovered that love is the more excellent way (1Corinthians 12:31).

Amelia also knew of a *JOY* which is inexpressible and full of glory. (1Peter 1:8) It has been said that "Joy is the flag that flies over our heart to show that the King of Kings is in residence today!" The joy we have in Jesus is not governed by our situation, and Amelia chose not to spend her time complaining about her circumstances. When I would ask how she was really feeling, she would quickly tell me of the difficulties she was experiencing, but would follow this with praise to the Lord that things were not any worse. She continued to think of others, and would tell of someone she knew who was having a more difficult time than herself. She kept the J-O-Y priorities in line: Jesus, Others, Yourself.

How could she remain filled with joy in the midst of her adversity? Her joy was in Christ. The King of Kings was in residence in her life. In John 15:11, Jesus said, *"These things I have spoken to you, that My joy may remain in you, and that your joy may be full."* How could she remain so strong when she was so ill and too weak to even care for herself? She remained strong because the joy of the Lord was her strength (Nehemiah 8:10).

I was with her one day when a lady asked how she could keep such a wonderful attitude with what she was facing. Her response was simply that she couldn't imagine handling it any other way. Amelia could relate to Paul as he was attempting to complete a journey he was taking in Acts 20:24. *"But none of these things move me; nor do I count my life dear to myself, so that I may finish my race with joy, and the ministry which I received from the Lord Jesus, to testify to the gospel of the grace of God."* Amelia finished her race with joy. Her life testified of the sufficiency of the grace of God.

One of my daily prayers for Amelia was that she would have *PEACE*. I had sensed an incredible peace during my brief storm, and I wanted her to experience that same unexplainable peace that passes all understanding. Peace is that supernatural calm that we can only experience in Christ. John 14:27 speaks of this peace of God. *"Peace I leave with you, My peace I give to you; not as the world gives do I give to you. Let not your heart be troubled, neither let it be afraid."* Philippians 4:7 reminds us that His peace will keep our hearts content as we trust in Him. The peace of God has often been compared to a serene body of water. An old hymn reminds us that our soul can have peace like a river. We know that there are times when a storm will approach, and the river can become turbulent. However, we can still know the peace of God during these times of turbulence, because He has promised to be with us. *"When you pass through the waters, I will be with you; And through the rivers, they shall not overflow you. When you walk through the fire, you shall not be burned, Nor shall the flame scorch you. For I am the LORD your God... " (Isaiah 43:2-3).*

Amelia never appeared troubled or afraid. She knew Jesus Christ personally, and *"He Himself is our peace" (Ephesians 2:14).* Jesus had calmed the storm in her life, and she was resting peacefully. Amelia had an incredible ability to keep her eyes focused on Jesus Christ rather than on the severity of her situation. She was able to reach out in faith each day and hold to God's unchanging hand. She was able to look with eyes of faith, and when she was physically weak, her faith was strong. She knew the peace speaker, so she did not have to fear the turbulent waters in her life. Jesus is the Prince of Peace. My prayer for peace was answered!

Amelia was able to remain patient and *LONGSUFFERING* throughout her storm. Patience is a trait that has to be developed through trials. We have no real need for patience when everything is going our way. It is when we find ourselves in situations we have no control over that we have the opportunity to develop patience.

When I was a student at the Medical College of Georgia in the mid-70's, counted cross stitch was becoming very popular. We had long days and nights of studying, and cross stitching became our outlet to get away from *Grant's Atlas of Anatomy* for a while. I still remember one little project I completed and framed. It said: "Patience is the ability to idle your motor, when you feel like stripping your gears!" There may have been days when Amelia felt like stripping her gears; there were certainly some days of frustration when I felt this way, but she remained able to idle her motor in the midst of the storm.

We all have dealt with impatience at one time or another. I am reminded of the person whose prayer for patience was, "Lord, give me patience, and give it to me now!" It usually doesn't come that easily. I have found that when I recognize a need to develop more patience in my life, I find myself in the longest, slowest line at the grocery store. Amelia was a well organized person who usually had everything under control, yet she demonstrated such peace and patience as she allowed God to work out His plan throughout her illness. *"I waited patiently for the LORD, and He inclined to me, And heard my cry. He also brought me up out of a horrible pit, Out of the miry clay, And set my feet upon a rock, And established my steps. He has put a new song in my mouth- Praise to our God; many will see it and fear, And will trust in the LORD" (Psalm 40:1-3). "But those who wait on the Lord Shall renew their strength; They shall mount up with wings like eagles, They shall run and not be weary, They shall walk and not faint" (Isaiah 40:31). "The Lord is good to those who wait for Him, To the soul who seeks Him" (Lamentations 3:25). "But let patience have its perfect work, that you may be perfect and complete, lacking nothing" (James 1:4).* Amelia did all she could do in her situation, and then she was able to sit back, relax, and leave the rest to God. Her ability to show patience actually showed her tremendous faith and trust in God. She had made a choice to honor Christ through the situation she faced. She chose to put on patience, not because of her circumstances, but because she had decided to follow Jesus. *"Therefore, as the elect of God, holy and beloved, put on tender mercies, kindness, humility, meekness, longsuffering" (Colossians 3:12).* She remained able to display that gentle, peaceful spirit which is precious in the sight of God. *"Do not let your adornment be merely outward- arranging the hair, wearing gold, or putting on fine apparel- rather let it be the hidden person of the heart, with the incorruptible beauty of a gentle and quiet spirit, which is very precious in the sight of God" (I Peter 3:3-4).*

Amelia also demonstrated her love for Christ by displaying the fruits of *KINDNESS, GOODNESS,* and *GENTLENESS* to others when there was nothing to gain in return. Even when our circumstances do not seem to be good, God is still good. Because she had experienced the goodness of God in her life, she desired to cultivate the fruits of kindness, goodness, and gentleness. Amelia was not a prideful lady who felt a need to outwardly adorn herself, and she truly demonstrated the more desirable hidden beauty.

During the last few weeks of her life, I talked with old friends and neighbors who dropped in to check on her. I enjoyed talking with them as they shared stories of their memories of Amelia. One gentleman who had grown up with Amelia, and had also been her neighbor for many years, shared several stories of her kindness. I was interested to hear him share about knowing Amelia in high school. He related that she was a beautiful young lady who was also highly intelligent. In later years, he related that he had a difficult time reading and understanding legal documents he would receive regarding his property. He would bring them up to Amelia, and she would read over the documents. Then she would explain their contents and advise him of how they should be handled. One lady shared that Amelia had sent her a book in an attempt to give her some medical advice about some problems she was experiencing.

During her last year of teaching, Amelia was required to complete a computer course that was mandatory for all teachers. She barely had the energy for a full day of school, yet was also taking this course in the evening. She had started the class the year before and had been unable to complete it due to her illness. Therefore, she already was familiar with some of the initial material being covered. She could have quickly completed her assignment and been on her way home. However, she noticed the teacher sitting beside her was having difficulty with the task. She chose to stay, and assisted her in completing the assignment that evening. They were from different schools and did not know each other at the time. It was only later that they made a connection. The teacher Amelia had chosen to stay and help that evening was my sister! We called that another one of our interesting coincidences.

Amelia also frequently showed kindness and goodness to a neighbor who lived a simple life. He was self-sufficient for his basic needs, but was unable to read or write. He was fearful and untrusting of some people, but he trusted Amelia and depended on her to help him with personal business matters he could not understand.

How did she find the strength to minister to others with the great needs she had? I believe the answer to this question is found in Psalm 23. *"The LORD is my shepherd; I shall not want. He makes me to lie down in green pastures; He leads me beside the still waters, He restores my soul; He leads me in the paths of righteousness For His name's sake. Yea, though I walk through the valley of the shadow of death, I will fear no evil; For You are with me; Your rod and Your staff, they comfort me. You prepare a table before me in the presence of my enemies; You anoint my head with oil; My cup runs over. Surely goodness and mercy shall follow me all the days of my life; And I will dwell in the house of the LORD Forever."* Kindness, gentleness, goodness, and mercy did follow Amelia all the days of her life. She will dwell in the house of the Lord forever!

Amelia remained *FAITHFUL* to all the important commitments in her life. She might have grown tired and weary, but she chose to fight the good fight. She might have felt like giving up, but she chose to keep the faith. *"I will sing of the mercies of the Lord forever; With my mouth will I make known Your faithfulness to all generations" (Psalm 89:1).* How could she remain so faithful to her commitments in the midst of such adversity? She could be faithful because God was faithful (1Corinthians 1:9). She could remain faithful because she knew that God's word was true and His faithfulness was unending. *"Forever, O LORD, Your word is settled in heaven. Your faithfulness endures to all generations..." (Psalm 119:89-90).* She remembered the promise of Revelation 2:10. *"...Be faithful until death, and I will give you the crown of life."*

Amelia was faithful to her family and friends. She continued to show love and concern for them. She was thoughtful of how her illness impacted them and tried to make decisions and handle situations in a way that would be easier for everyone.

She remained faithful to her job for as long as she possibly could. She was concerned about disrupting the schedule and routine of her school children who needed structure and consistency to learn. She tried to schedule appointments in Atlanta late in the afternoon so that she did not miss classroom instruction. Her school schedule was always foremost in her mind as she worked out her chemotherapy schedule.

Amelia was faithful to her church for as long as possible during her illness. She had a tremendous love and attitude of gratitude for her church. She pushed herself to be there when she often did not feel well, because she found love, joy, strength, and encouragement there. After a long hard day at school, she would go back to church on Wednesday evening to assist in filling guest bags for Sunday services. She remained faithful to her commitment to be a choir member for as long as she could. She attended choir practice sessions and was even able to be a part of the choir recording that was completed during her illness. She didn't physically feel up to spending these additional hours at the church after working all day, but she didn't want to miss the spiritual blessing she knew she would receive from being there. God used her faithfulness to challenge those around her to be more firmly committed to the cause of Christ, and we were all encouraged and strengthened by her faithfulness to her commitments. *"I have not hidden Your righteousness within my heart; I have declared Your faithfulness and Your salvation; I have not concealed Your lovingkindness and Your truth From the great assembly" (Psalm 40:10).*

God doesn't promise the way will always be easy, but He does promise that following Him will be worth it. I am sure Amelia agreed that is was worth it all when she finally saw Jesus face to face! She ran the race with such courage and faith. She finished well!

I believe the fruit of *SELF-CONTROL* is developed much like the fruit of patience. Self-control is developed through trials and pressures that accompany them. We have little need for self-control when everything is under control. How we handle a situation when the storms rage measures our level of self-control. Self-control is the discipline of self, so that we are able to live and respond in the spirit, rather than living and responding in the flesh. It is the ability to remain joyful when we are not in a pleasant situation. It is the ability to remember that we are more than conquerors through Him who loved us, and to live like a conqueror spiritually when we are fighting a losing battle physically.

How can we maintain a spirit of self-control when we recognize we are in a situation over which we have no control? We can do this because we are reminded in Philippians 4:13 that *"I can do all things through Christ who strengthens me."* Amelia had learned to trust that God was in control, and when His plan was not her plan, His plan was the perfect plan. *"For My thoughts are not your thoughts, Nor are your ways My ways,"* says the Lord. *"For as the heavens are higher than the earth, So are My ways higher than your ways, And My thoughts than your thoughts"* (Isaiah 55:8-9).

The first time I went with Amelia for a chemotherapy treatment, a doctor who was conducting a clinical trial approached Amelia about participating in his study. Another patient spoke with her about her involvement in the clinical trials. Amelia seemed uninterested in this and stated that she lived too far away to make a weekly trip in to Atlanta. I assured her that if she felt she wanted to try this, transportation could be arranged, yet she seemed perfectly content with what was being done. After discontinuing the last of the chemotherapy treatments she tried, someone talked with her about another program they had heard about trying when conventional treatment had not been successful. Again, she showed no interest in this. She had learned to be content in her situation, and she was at peace with where she was and where she was going. Many people facing her crisis try multiple approaches to treatment in their attempt to find a cure. Amelia felt no need to do this, and she was able to maintain self-control when things did not go as we had hoped and planned. She was able to idle her motor and wait for God to work His perfect plan in her life.

Amelia did not talk about the severity of her condition and her helplessness to change the course it was taking. She never expressed fear of cancer or of dying. God had removed all fear and replaced it with love, power, and a sound mind. She maintained the spirit of calmness and self-control till the very end of her journey. She was able to do this because she recognized that God was the source of her strength and the strength of her life. She was able to maintain self-control because she knew that God was in control!

Amelia worked hard at everything she had committed herself to do. She was a lady of small stature, but she had one of those take charge personalities. However, she became able to take a step back, let God take charge, and have His perfect will and way in her life. She allowed God to use the adversity in her life to shape her character into the character of Christ. *"Therefore let those who suffer according to the will of God commit their souls to Him in doing good, as to a faithful Creator"* (I Peter 4:19). She was indeed ambitious, industrious, hardworking, beloved, and a worker for the Lord. Amelia's name had been well chosen for her.

Chapter Eleven

THE JOURNEY

"**J**anuary 23, 2002-the day the symptoms of my cancer began."
(*Amelia's Journal*) Amelia shared with me that she had been having some gastrointestinal problems for some time, and had tried
to treat them with over-the-counter medications. She got up this
particular morning and had severe diarrhea. She was scheduled to
attend a school-related workshop that day and did not feel she
needed to miss it. She went to the workshop and felt very bad all
day. She came home and scheduled an appointment with her general practitioner. Prescription medications did not resolve her
problems, and she returned to her doctor. Thankfully, he became
suspicious that much more was going on than gastrointestinal
problems, and he ordered the initial CA-125 blood test. This is
apparently not a test typically ordered by a general practitioner.
In fact, some ladies have related they have had a difficult time
convincing their gynecologist to order this test. When the test
results were received, the CA-125 level was significantly ele-
vated, and she was immediately referred to her local
gynecologist. It is important to note that she had seen her gynecologist for her yearly physical several months earlier, and
everything had appeared to be fine. Her Pap smear had been normal, but unfortunately, the Pap smear is not an effective method
for detecting ovarian cancer. After reviewing her current symptoms and lab results of the CA-125 test, he quickly made
arrangements for her to have an appointment with the gynecologic oncologist in Atlanta. Amelia told me that on Friday of that

week, she was so sure she had a serious medical problem and would not be back to school on Monday, that she left extended lesson plans for her students.

"By March 1ˢᵗ, I was on the operating table- ovarian cancer Stage III-C. My family and I knew it was cancer before the surgery. We were calm- prayerful- but in shock! My immediate family was at the hospital with me- my Dad, 85 at the time. His minister brought him up and took care of him. My daughter and son-in-law, and members of my loving extended family that I married into were there. Thankfully, they didn't divorce me when I divorced my husband. Their love and support have been unwavering. My cousin was there. I am always thankful for the love and support her family has given to me. Patty, our minister of music, and Donna, wife of the assistant pastor, were there." (Amelia's Journal)

After Amelia's initial surgery, the gynecologic oncologist told her family that he was able to remove 95% of the cancer. She would have six chemotherapy treatments, one every three weeks, of Taxol and Carboplatin. Her first chemotherapy treatment was scheduled for March 26, 2002.

March 26, 2002

Dear Amelia,

I was so excited to see you at church on Sunday! You look wonderful! We've come a long way in a short time, haven't we? I pray for you daily, but you were especially on my mind today. The Lord has just placed a very special love and concern in my heart for you. I believe if I understood you correctly that today would be your first treatment. When I woke up this morning, that was on my mind, and I prayed for you before I got out of bed. I believe so strongly in the power of prayer. Prayer truly does change things! I believe that God chooses different ways to bring about our healing, but His ways and His plans are always perfect. His grace is sufficient for our every need! What a great Heavenly Father we have!

I feel so unworthy of the great gift of healing that He chose for me, and I am committed to use this situation to glorify and exalt His name. I've been able to share my story with so many people already. Even in the doctor's office on my last visit, we were able to share with people in the waiting area about God's great blessing to us. Someone asked my husband about my situation after I was called back into the doctor's office. This gave him the opportunity to share about how blessed we had been with the non-malignant diagnosis. One lady was sitting there reading a Bible, and she and my husband continued to share about the goodness of the Lord. He noted that another lady only listened and appeared a bit uncomfortable with their conversation. He feared she didn't know the Lord and was facing this huge mountain alone.

As much as I wish you were not facing these chemotherapy treatments, I do believe that God chooses to heal us in different ways. I do believe your healing will be complete, and you will soon be as good as new! I also believe that because God has chosen this path for you, that you will be given many opportunities to share with others and exalt His name through this. We were made to praise Him, and I just know that you are going to have so many opportunities to share your experience with others. You are going to come in contact with many people you would have otherwise never met, and some of them may have never heard the good news of Jesus Christ. We never know what a life-changing impact we can have on someone by simply sharing our story of what the Lord has done, and is doing for us!

Amelia, I prayed specifically this morning that the joy of the Lord would be your strength during this time. My mind also went back again to the fourth chapter of Philippians, which is one of my favorites. I pray that you will be anxious for nothing, and that the peace of God, which surpasses all understanding, will guard your heart and mind through Christ Jesus. I'm so glad that my God shall supply ALL YOUR NEED according to his riches in glory by Christ Jesus. While I've been home recuperating I've had more time to spend in God's word, and daily I am amazed at how it comes alive for me with promises I can claim for my present situation. We serve an awesome God! He made possible the bond we now share. In God's family, there are no strangers; only brothers and sisters we haven't yet met. I'm so glad He allowed me to meet you!

Please know that you will continue to be in my thoughts and prayers daily, especially during this time that you are going through your treatments. I'll be keeping up with you! Remember, I'm cheering you on!!!

In Christ,
Luanne

Amelia experienced the typical side effects of weakness, neuropathy, and sores in her mouth. She lost her hair after the first treatment, but she was not at all bothered by this. She never got a wig because she felt it would be too hot and bothersome. She said her cancer insurance policy would have provided for a wig, but it would have just been a waste of their money. The ladies of her choir gave her a hat party as soon as she felt able to return to church. She got some beautiful hats, but sometimes chose to wear nothing on her head, because she said they just made her hot. She noted that when she would go out in public she would get strange looks, especially from the children. Then she remembered she obviously looked like a woman, but she had no hair! She also lost some of her nails. She commented that having hair didn't make her feel feminine, but having fingernails did. When she felt stronger, she enjoyed going for a manicure and having acrylic nails applied to her very thin fingernails.

On July 9, 2002, Amelia was scheduled for her sixth and final chemotherapy treatment. This was the first time I had been able to take her. I knew she had friends and co-workers who had volunteered to go with her, but I insisted I wanted to go with her. I knew this would give me several hours to spend with her, and I really wanted to get to know her better. I also wanted to have the opportunity to experience a day at the infusion center. I wanted a close-up view of what Amelia had been going through, and I knew it would be another reminder for me of how blessed I had been to be spared this dreadful disease.

I sat attentively by her side for six hours that day, holding her hand and praying for a miracle. It was the longest time we had actually spent together, and this gave us a perfect opportunity to learn more about each other. As we left the infusion center that day, Amelia closed the door, gave me a big hug, lifted her hands into the air, and praised God for seeing her through those six long and difficult treatments.

A second-look surgery was scheduled for September 6, 2002. The continued decline of the CA-125 level was a good indicator that the chemotherapy had been successful in destroying the cancer cells that had remained after the initial surgery, but this would allow the oncologist to view the area and confirm that healing had occurred. We had reason to be optimistic at this point.

August 28, 2002

Dear Amelia,

I was so glad to see you again on Saturday. You look great, and I'm so glad you're finally getting enough energy back to do a few things again. And your hair!!! I was so excited to see your hair, eyebrows, and eyelashes returning!!! This is just an outward sign of inner healing. God does give us signs that He is involved in our lives. I believe this is one of those signs for you, a sign of new life, like new flowers popping through the ground in the springtime! I praise God for this and the sign that He is at work in your life!

I am so glad you have finally gotten things scheduled for your second-look surgery. Sitting around waiting and not knowing anything can be so stressful. You've done more than enough of that over the past few weeks. I know this has to be an anxious time for you now as you wait and wonder about this upcoming surgery. I won't try to tell you not to worry, because I've done more than my share of that when I've faced things much less serious than what you've been enduring. It's part of our human nature that kicks in. What I will say is to just try to lean on the strong arms of Jesus and draw strength from Him during these few more days of waiting. I remember as a child, one of the first verses I ever learned was Psalm 56:3. "What time I am afraid, I will trust in Thee." The more I have learned to trust Him, the easier it has become to trust Him in those situations over which I have no control. When we realize that He is all we've got, we find that He is all we need! "My grace is sufficient for you, for My strength is made perfect in weakness. Therefore most gladly I will rather boast in my infirmities, that the power of Christ may rest upon me" (II Corinthians 12:9). Can you even imagine trying to go through this without God's love, mercy, grace, and faithfulness in your life? We are so blessed to be His children!

Satan knows that my heart forever belongs to God, and he can't change that, but he often tries to attack me through my mind and thoughts. He is the source of our fears and causes us to worry and doubt. I pray that if he tries this trick with you, you will be able to resist him through the power of Jesus Christ that is within you. "For God has not given us a spirit of fear, but of power and of love and of a sound mind" (II Timothy 1:7). One strategy that has been tried and proven true for me is Philippians 4:8. "...Whatever things are true, whatever things are noble, whatever things are just, whatever things are pure, whatever things are lovely, whatever things are of good report, if there is any virtue and if there is anything praiseworthy- Meditate on These Things!" When I find that I am thinking negative thoughts, I try to change my thought pattern to something that is good and worthy of praise. It really does work! We have the power to defeat the enemy and his tactics because the one who lives within us is greater than he who is in the world!

I continue to pray that you will "be anxious for nothing" and that "the peace of God, which surpasses all understanding, will guard your hearts and minds through Christ Jesus" (Philippians 4:6-7). How blessed we are to be able to call upon the name of *the Lord! "The name of the Lord is a strong tower; The righteous run to it and are safe" (Proverbs 18:10). "For You have been a shelter for me, A strong tower from the enemy" (Psalm 61:3). "How precious is your lovingkindness, O God! Therefore the children of men put their trust under the shadow of Your wings!" (Psalm 36:7). "Be merciful to me, O God; be merciful to me! For my soul trusts in You; And in the shadow of Your wings I will make my refuge, Until these calamities have passed by" (Psalm 57:1). I am praying that He will be so near that you will sense the presence of His wings around you until this is all over! He hasn't brought you this far to leave you now!*

Someone once said, "Do not fear tomorrow, for God is already there!" I am encouraging you not to fear September 6, because God is already there! That is an awesome thought! Our God is an awesome God! He loves you so much, and He is holding you safely in His strong arms. I'll talk with you before September 6, and I'll be praying for you daily between now and then!

I love you,
Luanne

The oncologist could not have been more pleased with what things looked like when he took the second look. He verbalized to us that things looked even better than he would have expected. We could not have been more pleased with the good news he gave us that day. We had reason to believe Amelia was going to do well.

She was still weak, but was regaining her strength. She knew she would not be able to return to school at the beginning of August, so arrangements were made for a long- term substitute teacher to take her class. Amelia did not care for television, but she enjoyed reading. She spent a great deal of time reading during this period of regaining strength and stamina. She finally told me one day that she thought she might enjoy watching some movies. I was not at all surprised to learn that she liked the old musicals, so I took up quite a few of those, as well as some Christian music videos. What did surprise me was that she also said she would like to see the *Star Trek* and *Star Wars* movies that my husband enjoys. Bryan and I do not share the same interest in movies, so he was delighted to find another lady who was interested in his movies. We enjoyed frequent visits at her home during the remainder of summer break before I had to return to work.

I had read everything I could find on the Internet regarding ovarian cancer. I knew the survival rate is between two and five years for someone who has a recurrence within the first year. It was February, and we were optimistic that we were going to make it past the one-year mark. Amelia went in for her routine mammogram during this month.

"In February of 2003 I went in for a routine mammogram. They kept me to do a magnification. I was scared! I've had two breast biopsies done- one in 1976- another in 1991. Both were benign. Thank God! But this came on the heels of cancer. The same week as the mammogram I had a blood test done- CA-125 to check my cancer, as I had been regularly doing. As it turned out, I didn't think too much or worry about the mammogram for a long while. I eventually learned that whatever is there is okay for now. The CA-125 was up. I was on my way to the hospital for another scan. Two spots showed up- one in the abdomen-lymph node, another next to my liver. Ovarian, as I knew, has a VERY high recurrence rate." (Amelia's Journal)

Amelia had begun to feel that something was not quite right. She felt very strongly that the body does indeed have biorhythms, and she tried to stay in tune with how she was feeling. She was again experiencing a bloating sensation and gastrointestinal disturbances. Our hopes of making it past the one year mark were beginning to shatter.

"I went to Piedmont for a needle biopsy on March 18th. Kim and Donna were there. That was on a Tuesday. By Friday, we had the results- ovarian again. During my first doctor visit after this, he found signs of the cancer in my lower colon that had not shown up on the scan. Scheduled for surgery April 10. God and all my angels continued to hold me up. Praise God for your faithfulness. You've helped me to stand, when without you and God, I

would have fallen in hopelessness. I thank and praise God for you all! Surgery April 10th- all my prayer warriors are at work- here- there- everywhere! Many of my angels are with me."
(Amelia's Journal)

We all anxiously and prayerfully sat in the surgical waiting area, waiting to hear from the doctor. He came out and was willing to meet with the entire group of prayer warriors who were there for her that day. We all squeezed into the little consultation room and were very anxious to hear how things had gone. He shared with us that he had gotten lemons that day, but was able to make lemonade! We tried to interpret that statement optimistically. He was able to remove the mass from the lymph node and liver, and also had removed twelve inches of the sigmoid colon. Recovery would prove to be much more difficult than the initial surgery had been.

Amelia was in a great deal of pain when she was brought up to her hospital room. She looked up at me with weak and anxious eyes and said, "I hurt." It was so painful for me to hear those words and feel so helpless to make things better. I wanted so badly to take away her pain, but I couldn't. Fortunately, I could whisper a prayer to the One I knew was able to do those things for her that I could not. Once again, those feelings of guilt and helplessness rushed over me. Why was she having to suffer like this when I had been spared? I stayed at the hospital that afternoon until she finally appeared to be comfortable. Kim was staying with her that night, and I would return to stay with her another night while she was there. Amelia remained comfortable the rest of that night, but was unable to sleep at all. She described the spiritual experience she had that night.

"With the help of all my prayer warriors, I was lifted up to the mountaintop that morning and didn't come down until the next morning when the hospital rudely decided to check all their disaster drill alarms right outside my room. I didn't sleep all night. I communed with God! The nurse came in often to check on me. Kim slept. The nurse asked me the next morning if I'd slept any at all. She mentioned that every time she came in I was

wide awake. I was buoyed up on the wings of prayer! That was the first time I've ever felt so loved! If you've never been there, I simply don't have words to describe it." (Amelia's Journal)

It was soon time to begin six more chemotherapy treatments. This time, Doxil was the chosen treatment. After the first chemotherapy treatment, she found out that in rare cases, Doxil has caused damage to the heart muscle and can actually lead to heart failure. Kim took her to the hospital for a cardiology consultation between the first and second treatment. We were grateful that everything checked out well with her heart, and the recommendation was to proceed with the Doxil treatments. The chemotherapy appeared to be even harder on her body this time. Her feet and hands developed a reddened and burned appearance and were very sensitive. The skin would peel, and she had a difficult time finding shoes she could tolerate. She also developed these red and irritated patches over her entire trunk. She suffered from anemia and was extremely weak, even with weekly Procrit shots. We felt the Procrit commercials we had seen on television exaggerated the results a bit.

"I lost twelve inches of colon during surgery and had a little more trouble right after coming to my room than I did after the first surgery. But I was soon up and about- slowly. But praise God, still alive! Six more chemo treatments- a lot harder on my body this time- anemia- even taking Procrit shots every week. But God be praised—September, CAT scan clear- no sign of cancer. I was still anemic, couldn't stand for longer than five minutes." (Amelia's Journal)

Amelia was cancer-free again, and we had much for which to be thankful! We encouraged her to be as active as possible and try to regain her strength. We also tried to encourage good nutrition, because the side effects of the chemotherapy, coupled with the loss of part of the colon during the second surgery, had made food tolerance an issue. It was during this time that we started going out to eat weekly. Applebee's became our weekly meeting place. While good nutrition was healing to her body during this time, I believe her heart and soul were finding strength and healing as well. We would sit for hours, and she would share things about her past that were on her mind. She was able to share so openly and honestly with me, not because she was proud of everything she had done, but because she was so proud of what God had done to transform her life.

"Luanne and I have a spiritual connection ordained by God. I see and feel the Holy Spirit at work in myself when I'm with her. She gives me that funny little half smile of hers, and I know I'm doing the God thing again. Applebee's has become our favorite haunt. I think they know us on sight by now. We are the two ladies who come in to eat- and stay forever just talking. That's what it looks like to them. We're really having church- they just don't realize it." (Amelia's Journal)

The Holy Spirit was indeed at work in Amelia's life, strengthening and sustaining her, and giving her the courage to persevere. She started singing in the church choir again, and once again went to church early on Wednesday evenings to help fill guest bags that would be given to visitors in the Sunday services. She did continue to fatigue rather easily and was concerned about being strong enough to return to a full day at school.

"I was worried at this point that I might not be able to go back to school. Why do I still take back my worry when I firmly and confidently know that God will take care of me? Still human, not perfect- God still loves me anyway. I returned to work on November 17th- with much praise to God and 24 hour prayer from all my warriors, as is still happening today to keep me going. I wouldn't be here today without you and God. It's all about Him- not me! I need to be reminded of that often. We shouldn't sweat the small stuff, and remember, it's all small stuff compared to where we will spend eternity." (Amelia's Journal)

Amelia returned to work on November 17, 2003. This was indeed another answered prayer for her and all of us. She loved teaching the school children, and was hoping to be able to do so for several more years. It was now Thanksgiving, and the timing could not have been more appropriate to give thanks for another gift of strength and healing. I was so delighted to receive a beautiful Thanksgiving card from Amelia. Inside this card she had written…

YOU'RE A BLESSING TO ME
"I'm thankful everyday I live,
for the warmth and kindness that you give.
Thankful that in God's design,
He planned it so your path crossed mine!"

It was during this time that her church choir was also rehearsing for a recording of a new church choir music book. Amelia was able to participate in this recording, going for evening practices after teaching school all day. We were so thankful that she was able to be a part of this project. I was worried she was pushing herself too hard and not getting enough rest. However, this was such a very special blessing for her, and God obviously intervened and gave her the added strength she needed in order to do this. In our weakness, He truly is strong.

At this same time, the principal at Amelia's school was also a pastor at a small church in the area. What a blessing he was to Amelia. She shared with joy about the times she was able to go by his office and share with him about the goodness of God in her life. He was high on her angel list. His church had also been so faithful to pray for Amelia. He had asked her to come and speak at this church on a Sunday morning in January of 2004, and I went with her that day. It was the first time she had spoken to a group about her illness, and she was a bit apprehensive about speaking publicly. *"I think my principal must have taken unfair advantage of me in a very weak moment of recovery from chemo. Surely I would not have agreed to this torture if I had been well. Any of us who have known him for oh, say a day, know how he works and maneuvers us where he thinks we need to be. He chats, jokes, plants the seed, hems you up and all of a sudden, his idea becomes yours. We laugh, but I believe that he is another one of my angels that God has sent to me, to show me the way home. I know this will become a pleasant remembered experience, if I can just live through it. Haven't we all been there? Whether it's a life-*

altering experience or just an everyday annoyance. We pray for it to just be over and then we can go back to being thankful. But not while we're suffering... Too much to ask of us. I believe that this is one of the many messages that God has given to me, and it has taken two years of living with cancer for me to really listen to Him." (Amelia's Journal)

It was a cold, crisp Sunday morning, and the drive out to this little country church was beautiful. The scenic drive through meadows and fields was not the only beautiful thing we experienced that morning. On the way over, Amelia and I were singing along with the practice disc of the music she was learning for the choir recording. The song, *Spirit of the Living God,* began to play. Amelia's soprano voice and my alto voice blended harmoniously to create a joyful noise unto the Lord as we petitioned this Spirit to fall fresh on us that morning. Our hearts were also joined in harmony, and she reached over to grasp my hand. The Spirit of this living God was very evident at that moment, and we sensed a strong presence and nearness of God. It was another one of those very special moments God had planned that we would share together. It was a time when we were reminded that we were children of God, and sisters by divine appointment.

Amelia spoke with such strength and courage that morning. She shared about the sufficiency of God's grace during her journey with cancer. What a powerful testimony she gave of how God had gone before her and prepared the way for this storm she would face. Each year during hurricane season, many people living in coastal communities must take action to protect their property and themselves from an oncoming storm. They will cover their windows, place sandbags in low areas to prevent flooding, and provide additional bracing and support to weaker structures. Likewise, a strong support system had been built before the diagnosis was given and the storm arrived in Amelia's life. She felt so blessed to have friends and family who had stood by her side night and day. She loved to talk about her angels that God had sent her way to lift her up and show her the way home. On our way home from this little church, Amelia commented that she saw me taking notes while she was speaking. I told her I was jotting down some things I would want to include in the book I was going to write about us someday!

We enjoyed time together during the holidays. She seemed to be feeling better than I had seen her during this entire ordeal. This was the first time she had been to our home. I offered to come and pick her up, but she said she felt up to the 45 minute drive. We spent the afternoon looking at our pictures from the mission trip in Europe. Then we enjoyed dinner and exchanged gifts.

Shortly after the holidays, Amelia went back to the doctor for routine blood work. The CA-125 had been slowly rising for several weeks and was now up to 300. The CA-125 blood test is not always accurate in the detection of ovarian cancer. However, it had proven over and over again to be a good tumor marker for Amelia. While the quantity of the number did not always necessarily correspond to the severity of the tumor growth, a rise in the CA-125 level consistently meant that there was a recurrence of the cancer somewhere. Another CT scan was ordered. On Saturday, before she was scheduled to return to the doctor the following Tuesday, she was the speaker for our ladies' luncheon at the church. Again, she did an excellent job of sharing about God's goodness throughout her battle. She also shared more information specifically about ovarian cancer, its symptoms, and her personal feelings about what may have contributed to her problem. As she was leaving that day, I gave her a hug and told her I would see her on Tuesday afternoon because I was going with her to the doctor. I suspected she would plan to go alone, as she didn't want to be a bother to anyone and knew everyone had busy schedules. My suspicions had been correct, but she expressed joy and relief that I would be with her. I had commented to several friends I knew were praying for her that unless God intervened, I felt sure we would get more bad news. She didn't need to have to hear it alone.

Our doctor came into the examining room that day, and as always, he greeted her with a hug. He did indeed have more bad news for us that day. How thankful I was that I had insisted on coming along. He explained that after you have had a recurrence with this disease, you treat it as a chronic illness. While you do expect there will be recurrences, you try to locate them quickly and treat them aggressively. There were new masses in the abdominal area, as well as on the liver and pancreas. There would be no more surgery, and this time the treatment of choice would be Gemzar. He told us we were going to love Gemzar. He related that the side effects were not usually as bad, and she probably would not lose her hair. Naturally, we took that very positively and prayed once again that this would be the treatment that would bring about the complete healing we continued to hope and pray for daily.

It was February and Amelia wanted so badly to be able to finish her school year without interruption. On the way home that day, we discussed how this might be arranged. She didn't know if she would be able to work while taking the chemotherapy treatments, but I insisted that she did not need to delay starting them. We figured that if she could get the first treatment during the next week, the second treatment would come on the Friday before the week of spring break. That week off would give her time to rest and recuperate from the second treatment. Then it would soon be time for summer break by the time the third treatment was scheduled. It sounded like a good plan, and indeed it was. She called the infusion center and was able to schedule her first treatment for the following Friday. Our plan was in place.

Before I left her that day, I reminded her of the *Footprints In The Sand* poem. This poem explains that as we journey through this life, we are never alone. There will always be two sets of footprints in the sand, because Christ is always by our side. However, during times of great adversity, we may notice that there is only one set of footprints. During those times, Christ will be carrying us. I explained further to Amelia that even during those times of great difficulty in her life when Christ was actually carrying her, there would still be two sets of footprints in the sand. The other set would be mine!

3-28-03

Dear Amelia,

I've been meaning to send you a note for two weeks and just never seemed to be able to get it together. Maybe it's because I would find this card that does a much better job of saying what I wanted to say. Basically, I just want you to know that I promise I'll be there for you!

Your latest reports are certainly not what I had prayed for, hoped for, and believed. I always try to be optimistic and find the positive in every situation I encounter. I sometimes worry that people will think I'm minimizing the problem at hand. I pray that I never come across that way with you. I realize that this is a very serious problem that we are facing. I just know that God is bigger than all our problems. I know that His ways are not always our ways, nor are His plans always our plans, but I know that His ways are higher than ours. I know that He has plans for us, and His plans are to give us a hope and a future, and not to harm us. I know that His plans for our life are based on His great love for us and are always in our best interest. I know that His grace is sufficient for all our needs. I know that His stedfast love never ceases. I know that His mercies never cease and are new every morning. I know that He can give us peace that passes all understanding. I know that His joy can be our strength. I know that when we are weak, He is strong! I know that He can hide us under the shelter of His wings until each calamity that we must face has passed. I know that He can heal us of all our diseases. I know that Jesus Christ is the same yesterday, today, and forever. I know that what He has done before, He can surely do again. I know that trials will come our way, and they come to make us stronger in Him. My optimism in this trial that we now face, and every other trial that we face, is based on what I know of His character from His word and from my personal experiences of His faithfulness. I know that He is able to do exceedingly, abundantly above all that we could ask or think, according to His power at work in us. This is why I am optimistic! This is the reason for the hope that is within me! If God says it, we can believe it!

I must be honest and admit that I have had some discouraging moments over your latest test results. I've experienced some anxiety, disappointment, and frustration. I've cried just trying to tell my friends about it. I've asked the why and what if questions. I know that God is love, and sometimes wonder why He does allow us to face these storms, although I really know the answer. I've wondered why you're having to go through all of this difficulty, and I was spared. Yes, I've been down at times, but I just refuse to stay there.

I believe the message God has been speaking to me is for us to stay focused on Him. The reason I believe this is because this message keeps coming back to me. This was the essence of our Sunday School lesson last Sunday. We talked about the fact that when we focus on our problems, we have taken our focus off God, the solution to our problems. I am also reading a book now entitled "The Reason for My Hope" by Dr. Charles Stanley. Then yesterday, one of my therapist friends at work called me at 11:30 to see if we could meet for lunch. The interesting thing about her calling was that morning as I was coming to work, she came to mind, and I thought how I wished I'd called her the night before to see if we could meet for lunch. I know God was at work in this encounter. She has been concerned about a number of things and just needed to talk and get another perspective on her problems and their possible solutions. I was able to share this same message about staying focused with her. We must keep our focus on the One who can solve our problems. When we can do this, the problems don't seem nearly as big as when we were focused on them. Christ must be the center of our attention and focus.

Amelia, I've been so encouraged and strengthened by your strong, brave spirit and your ability to be so positive through all these trials and difficulties that you have faced, and are now facing again. It has been such an inspiration to me and so many others to see this consistency in you. I'm sure you've had some

down times, as we are all human and these are normal reactions
to difficult situations. What I want you to know is that if and when
these times come, I want to be there for you. I want to be an
encourager. Please don't ever hesitate to call me, even if it's just
to say, "This is a tough day, please pray a little harder!" I don't
want you to go through those times alone. I know that God
brought us together, and I know that He did it for a specific rea-
son. I want to help you get through this new trial, and we will!
I've got two ears for listening, two shoulders to cry on, two knees
to fall on in prayer, and two arms to wrap around you and remind
you that you are loved, and you are not alone. This is not the road
we would have ever chosen, but we will make it! I promise I'll be
there for you! God loves you so much, and so do I!

Luanne

Amazingly, she was able to make it through the first two
treatments and continue teaching until the school year ended in
late May. She had achieved an important goal that we had set, and
we felt that another prayer had been answered. Our doctor had
told us in the beginning that with Gemzar it is not uncommon to
have several treatments before the CA-125 level begins to drop.
Unfortunately for us, it never dropped at all. In fact, it continued
to slowly rise during the course of these treatments. Amelia
seemed to experience all the unfortunate side effects as well. She
again developed sores in her mouth, skin rash, fatigue, and anemia. Additionally, she had no appetite, no taste of food, and
began to experience nausea and vomiting. She was obviously
retaining abdominal fluid and could not breathe well unless she
was sitting upright. She was hospitalized for two days during
July, and four liters of fluid were removed from her abdomen.

My husband and I went up to visit her during this hospitalization. She immediately felt some relief after the fluid was
removed and was able to breathe better. She related her experience in the department where this procedure had been performed.
The technologist there had been playing the soundtrack to
Sleepless in Seattle, and Amelia commented that she enjoyed lis-

tening to that music so much. She liked those old songs such as Gene Autry's *Back in the Saddle Again.* We asked her if there was anything we could get for her that day. She usually couldn't think of anything she needed. However, she said she would really like to have a disc of that music to enjoy when she returned home. We were so pleased to find a copy for her later that evening, and took it to her when she returned home.

Unfortunately, the procedure to remove the excess fluid proved to be a very temporary measure. She soon began experiencing shortness of breath again. She stayed nauseated all the time and was not eating any solid foods. She drank milk, water, juice, and had ice chips. Her CA-125 continued to rise. After the fifth of six planned chemotherapy treatments with Gemzar, she and the doctor concluded that the treatments were not working. I was glad that Kim was taking her for this August appointment because I suspected some important decisions would need to be made. I had gone up the day before to assist her in getting a shower. After a few short steps with a walker into the bathroom and a quick shower, she was exhausted.

The doctor had determined that Gemzar had not been effective and that the abdominal tumors were creating a blockage that was contributing to all the gastrointestinal problems she was experiencing. He discussed with her that he could do more surgery to relieve these blockages and try another form of chemotherapy. While she never verbalized it, she was obviously growing tired and weary by this point. She decided she did not want to go through any more of these temporary measures. The chemotherapy treatments had rendered only temporary improvement and had been very hard on her body. The doctor talked with her about having someone stay with her, and she was resistant to that idea. She felt she could still be alone and preferred the quiet atmosphere of her home. She called me on her way home, but as usual, she tried to break the bad news softly. She said, "We've decided to stop the treatments for now and give my body some time to recover from all this chemo. Then we'll just see what happens and go from there!"

Amelia never discussed the fact that she knew she wasn't going to make it. However, she began to make plans to that effect. One afternoon I went up to visit, and when I walked into her bedroom she was sitting in her big chair. She pointed to the stool next to her and said, "Sit down, I need to talk to you!" When Amelia would say this, you just never knew what was coming next! Then she continued, "Kim will just die when she hears this, but I've been planning my service. I thought it would be easier on Kim just to go immediately to the cemetery and have a service. Then I want everyone to go back to the church and have a celebration service with lots of good singing. I've been planning all the songs I want to be sung, but I have decided that this is going to be so good, I want to be there! Have you ever heard of someone having their funeral service before they die?" This was the only time she ever mentioned dying to me. I had to quickly get my thoughts together before I responded. I told her there was a first time for everything and encouraged her to talk with her pastor and see how he felt about the idea.

The nausea continued, and she was growing weaker and weaker. On Saturday night, September 18, she fell during the night and was in the floor for several hours before she was finally able to reach a phone and call for help. She returned for her last doctor's appointment on September 21. It was obvious that her condition was deteriorating rapidly. While the Gemzar had clearly not been effective in reducing the tumor growth and lowering the CA-125 level, it appeared that it may have had some beneficial effect, because after discontinuing it, her overall decline was profound. On this last visit to her doctor, he told her he would have to make some decisions for her. He told her she absolutely could not be alone anymore. He also discussed the need to begin Hospice services. Then he sent her over to the hospital to have intravenous fluids to give her some nutritional support and hydration. She fell again that night as Kim and Donna were bringing her back into her house.

A schedule was developed and friends volunteered to be with her at all times. Hospice nurses began coming to her home. They brought medical equipment, including a hospital bed, bedside commode, and oxygen. They discussed the possible need to transfer her into a Hospice facility. The facility was over an hour from her home, so we prayed this would not become necessary. She loved her home so much and wanted to stay there. Being there would also be so much easier for Kim, who lived next door.

Each day, she seemed to become a little weaker. The last night that I stayed with her, she was unable to sleep at all. She could not breathe well lying down. She sat in the big chair, her dog Pepper slept on her bed, and I settled down on the hospital bed. It turned out to be another sleepless night, and I knew she was growing tired and weary in her race. I was reminded of a song Donna had shared with us...

THE OTHER SIDE
Turn down the day, turn out the light.
Quiet in the dark, another sleepless night.
Soft on the breeze a song in the night.
Feel the spirit rise with the morning.
Press on, oh tired and weary one.
You've done your best to stand when the day seems so long.
Press in, let worship be your guide,
to lead you through the night.
Your miracle will come on the other side of praise.
Raise up these arms, hold the banner high.
Surrender is the only way to life.

(Reprinted with permission of Brian Hardin.© 2001
Little China Music (sesac)., Lovella Music.)

Donna began staying every day during the week, and this was such a relief for Kim and Amelia. Donna feels a special calling to minister to people during their last days. She is so kind, soft-spoken, and compassionate. What a special blessing sent from above she was during this time! Donna assisted Amelia in working out all the final plans for her celebration service, and the date was scheduled for Thursday night, September 30. At one time during her illness, I had given Amelia a disc of old church hymns by the popular southern gospel trio, *Greater Vision.* She had listened to this music over and over. I dropped by to visit one day and found her crying. This was the third and last time I ever saw her cry. I immediately asked her what was wrong and she responded, "Oh, I'm all right. I just always cry when I hear this song." The title of the old hymn was *I Won't Have to Cross Jordan Alone.* She said she wanted my husband to sing this song at her celebration service, but she might need to audition him first. She had heard that he sang well, but she had never actually heard him sing. Amelia didn't get to audition Bryan before the service, but she trusted that he would do a good job for her. The choir would sing several of her favorite songs, a ladies trio would sing *The Potter's House,* and her pastor would speak. Amelia's condition was deteriorating so rapidly that we actually became concerned she might not make it till the date that service had been arranged. We would all encourage her to rest up for the big day she had planned, and her goal was to be strong enough to be there and enjoy her special service.

Unfortunately, when the big day arrived, it turned out to be the worst day Amelia had experienced. She realized by midday that there would be no way she could make it to the service. However, she talked with her pastor and said, "This is not about me, so I want you to go ahead and have the service tonight. I have lost friends and family who may be there, and I want them to know Jesus!" We dropped by her house on the way to the service, and indeed it had been a bad day. I knew she had to be incredibly sick to recognize she could not make it to this special service she had planned and anticipated for so long.

Arrangements were made to videotape the service so she could see it afterwards. It was a very special and touching experience, and was also an extremely emotional time for all of us who loved her so much. It would have been a difficult situation for us if she had been there or not. The special recliner chair that had been brought into the sanctuary for her was empty. Her not being able to attend just made us realize how near the end of her journey she really must be. After the music she had planned, her pastor spoke briefly and then shared Amelia's desire for everyone present to know about her Savior, and experience a personal relationship with Him as she did. After his remarks, he gave an invitation to those present to invite Christ into their lives. Nine people prayed to receive Christ as their personal Savior in the service that night. It truly had been a service of celebration. When we returned to Amelia's house to share the good news, she lifted her frail arm into the air and responded in her weak little voice, "Praise the name of the Lord!" The psalmist David expressed her sentiments in Psalm 63:4-8 when he said, *"Thus I will bless You while I live; I will lift up my hands in Your name. My soul shall be satisfied as with marrow and fatness, And my mouth shall praise You with joyful lips. When I remember You on my bed, I meditate on You in the night watches. Because You have been my help, Therefore in the shadow of Your wings I will rejoice. My soul follows close behind You; Your right hand upholds me."* I was reminded again of how well Amelia was living out the command of I Peter 4:16. *"Yet if anyone suffers as a Christian, let him not be ashamed, but let him glorify God in this matter."*

This was a very emotional night for me. I knew Amelia was critically ill when she did not make it to this special service. She had been so pleased with all the details she had planned for it. She knew it was going to be good, and she wanted so much to be there. Several people commented that night that we would all be back together very soon for the funeral service. I didn't accept that! I was honestly still clinging to the hope that she could be healed. I realize that God rarely chooses to work in this way today, but I also knew that with God, all things are possible (Mark 10:27). It was still possible that she could be well again! I concluded that Jesus had raised Lazarus from the dead and Hebrews 13:8 confirmed that *"Jesus Christ is the same yesterday, today, and forever."* It was still a possibility, and I continued to pray for that miracle!

She was growing obviously weaker each day. She continued to take her medications and ice chips by mouth. She was requiring more medication to be comfortable and was beginning to experience some confusion. We can now laugh as we remember Donna playing the celebration service videotape for her. Amelia loved music so much. She liked what she was hearing, but she had a little confusion about what group was actually singing on the tape. When she heard the trio singing, she thought that it was Diana Ross and the Supremes. Donna had a difficult time convincing Amelia she was not Diana Ross!

I dropped in for a short visit on Friday, and she was sleeping. I visited again on Sunday afternoon, and one of her church choir friends was sitting with her that afternoon. Amelia always wanted me to rub her feet and legs when I came. She thought I had the magic touch. After all, I was her own private therapist! As I sat there massaging her feet, she wanted me to tell her friend our story. I briefly shared the details of how we met, intentionally leaving out some details because I knew it would be too emotional to share. I didn't want to break Amelia's no crying rule. As I finished the details of our special story Amelia looked down at me and said, "Tell her the part about when you were sitting at your computer and God spoke to you. You left that part out!" I explained that I didn't know if I could get through that part, but after Amelia's "Oh, yes you can", I knew I could, and I did. We all had shed a few tears by the end of the story.

I visited again on Tuesday afternoon, October 4. Amelia had several visitors that afternoon, and she appeared somewhat confused and agitated. There seemed to be a more distant look in her eyes. She reached out for my hand and called me another friend's name. Kim called while I was there, and I stepped into another room to speak with her. I became emotional as I shared with Kim that she had not called my name when she saw me. I was devastated, and yet I felt so bad that I had been emotional with Kim. I should have been an encourager to her during this difficult time, yet she had to console me and reassure me that her mom knew who I was and that I was there by her side. The reality of the situation was hitting me hard, and it was such a painful reality to face.

For over two years when I had visited, we had this routine of saying hello and goodbye. I looked forward to ringing the doorbell, hearing Pepper begin to bark, and hearing Amelia making her way to the door. She had always greeted me at the door, given me a big hug followed by three little hugs and an accompanying, "I love you, love you, love you!" When I would leave, I would give her a big hug, a little kiss on the cheek, and say, "I've got to go now. I love you, and I'll see you again soon!" It was so difficult to come for a visit and know she would not meet me at the door. I remember the first day I visited after she told me she wasn't going to be able to come to the door. She had told me where the hidden key was located in the garage, but I couldn't find it. I had to call her on my cell phone and get further directions. With those organizational skills of hers, it was no problem. I had soon located the hidden key and was inside the house for my visit. It became more difficult and emotional to go through the goodbye routine as well.

I spoke with Kim on Wednesday and learned that Tuesday night had been a real challenge for them. The sitter had called during the night and asked Kim to come down to Amelia's house. Amelia had gotten up and walked into the kitchen, and the sitter could not get her to go back into the bedroom. When Kim arrived, her mom was very agitated and stated that she was doing her exercises. Amelia had not been up and ambulating for more than a week, yet Kim was amazed at the strength she demonstrated that night as she resisted their attempts to get her back into bed. The Hospice nurse described this episode to Kim as "terminal agitation". After this incident, they placed Amelia in the hospital bed where she remained until the end.

I came back to see her on Thursday and found her lying in the hospital bed for the first time. She often appeared to be sleeping. She did not speak at all, and when she did open her eyes, they had an even more distant look. How painful it was to see her in this condition. I battled tears the entire time I was there. I knew she was slowly slipping away from this life. I tried to leave three different times before I finally got courageous enough to stand by her bedside, hold her hand, and faintly whisper, "I've got to go now. I love you, and I'll see you again soon." Leaving from a visit had always been hard. She never wanted me to go and always insisted that I could stay a little longer. I was never really ready to leave either, but I always had a long drive home awaiting me. I fought back tears on the long drive home and prayed I would not have to see her in that condition again.

My family was planning to be in Athens for the University of Georgia football game over the weekend. We left on Friday afternoon to be with our son, who is a student there. Halfway through dinner, I remembered I had left my cell phone in the car. Seconds later, my husband's cell phone rang. My heart sank as I realized he was talking with Patty. I stepped outside the restaurant to talk with her. Amelia had taken a turn for the worse, and the Hospice nurse felt she probably wouldn't make it more than 24-48 hours. Patty told me if I wanted to see her again, I might need to make plans to come back home. I had a very difficult decision to make. I honestly did not want to see her again in that condition, and I had actually prayed the day before that I wouldn't have to see her again like that, yet I didn't want to walk away at the last minute and not be there for her. My heart was literally aching. I honestly did not know if I could bear to be there in the end. I did not know if my aching heart could take it. I had always thought of grief and heartache as an emotion, but I was feeling a real physical pain. What did I need to do? What a difficult decision to have to make. I told Patty I just needed some time to think about what I wanted to do, and that I would give them a call back.

Later on that evening, I called Amelia's house and Donna answered. She was there with Kim. Donna had been out of town all week and had just returned. It was as if Amelia was waiting for her to return. Donna sat by her bedside, holding her hand, and assuring her that all of us would be okay and that it was all right for her to leave us. I talked at length with Donna about the difficulty I was having in deciding whether to be there or not. I had really not addressed this issue before now, and I didn't know what I was going to do. I told her I honestly did not know if I could endure being there in the end, and I really meant that. I was so overcome with emotion that I felt as though my heart would literally break. Donna has such a sweet, quiet spirit, and yet an incredible strength during times like these. Once again, God had provided for every need. Donna assured me that she wanted to be there till the very end and understood my feelings if I didn't think I could be there. I was concerned that Kim would not understand and feel I was forsaking her mom during these final hours. I had promised in the beginning I was going to stand on the sidelines and cheer her all the way, yet now I felt like I was relinquishing on the commitment I had made. I also felt that I would be of no value to Kim at this time. I had already seen earlier in the week that Kim had to console me, rather than me being there to comfort her. I didn't need that to happen again. What a heartbreaking decision I had to make. I agonized on the phone with Donna for quite a while. We finally decided that I should stay in Athens overnight and make a decision by morning. I asked Donna to call me back if anything changed during the night.

I couldn't sleep at all. The pain felt so deep, and my heart was breaking. The journey was about to be over. I wasn't ready for it to end. I had not planned that it would end this way. I had planned to be on the sidelines, cheering her on as she fully recovered from this dreadful disease. At 1:10 a.m., my cell phone rang. It was Donna. She softly whispered, "She's gone."

Amelia had slipped away into the arms of her Heavenly Father. There was no fear, for she recognized these arms. They were the same strong arms that had supported and protected her throughout this entire ordeal. *"The eternal God is your refuge, And underneath are the everlasting arms..." (Deuteronomy 33:27).* My prayer for her complete healing had finally been answered. She had fully recovered from this dreadful disease. The race was over. Our incredible journey together had ended.

➤Chapter Twelve➤

BRAND NEW HOME

Amelia loved her home. It was her haven, her place of rest, peace, comfort, and security. After her divorce, she withdrew from many of her social activities as well as her church involvement. She built a new home on some of the large tract of land near Sand Hill that had belonged to her mother's family for many years. Amelia's mother lived there until her death in 1999, and her father remained there until his remarriage in 2004.

Amelia enjoyed her school staff and children, but she looked forward to coming home every afternoon to the quiet and solitude she found there after a busy, noisy day of school. Her dog, Pepper, was always glad to see her. They looked after each other well. Tending to Pepper was one of the first things on her agenda when she arrived home, and she did it well. Pepper was a light colored poodle that Amelia had taken in a few years earlier. Amelia feared that Pepper had previously been abused. She was fearful of strangers, particularly men. However, she loved Amelia and was always in her lap or near her side. Her loud bark alerted Amelia that someone was outside. They were a great pair, as they daily took care of each other.

Next, she would make a round through the house to check on all her plants. Amelia definitely had a green thumb. She also admitted to talking to her plants. I'm not sure what she said, but it must have worked! In her bay windows, there were picture perfect African violets that required daily nurturing. The small cuttings that she was rooting in the tiny glass vials also needed attention. Then she had to make sure the bird feeders outside were filled. I dropped by one Saturday afternoon to check on her and found her outside in her nightgown. She had not felt like getting dressed that day, but she had not neglected to look after those plants and animals that are a part of God's creation.

After all those after school activities were completed, she could grab a bite to eat and finally sit down in her blue recliner rocker in her family room. She needed to get off her feet, which were usually swollen. She had lots of problems with her feet, secondary to an old fracture and the neuropathy that developed as a side effect of the chemotherapy. She would reach for the latest book she was reading. She was always reading a good book, sometimes more than one at a time. Amelia's home was very dear to her. It was so quiet and so comfortable. It was truly a home, sweet home.

Amelia had chosen the design of her home when it was built back in 1986. She enjoyed showing me around her home and telling stories about various items that were especially dear to her. Her mother's round oak table and chairs remained in her kitchen. A unique old picture adorned the wall in the dining room. It had belonged to her grandmother and had been reworked several years earlier to preserve its quality and beauty. A beautiful childhood portrait of Kim hung over her bed, and she had a favorite picture of her mother hanging in her family room. She related to me that her mother had been her best friend, and had been there for her in the good times and the bad. She loved pictures of her family, and one wall of her family room was filled with these.

We even ventured up into the attic one day. Kim's baby bed and stroller were still there. A large and beautiful portrait of Amelia on her wedding day was lying nearby. She was a gorgeous young bride with dark hair and eyes. I recognized the smile on her face that day as being the same one I would see each time I was with her. And of course, there were the plastic freezer containers. There must have been hundreds of them! Amelia especially enjoyed telling me the stories of when she and her mom would freeze vegetables in the summer. Her favorite vegetable was the corn, which they cooked outside in a large wash pot over an open fire. Those were the good old days for Amelia.

Early in our friendship, she talked about how she wanted to get well quickly so she could come and see my home. We lived forty-five minutes apart, and she had not felt like venturing out that far, other than to those necessary medical appointments in Atlanta. I had shared memorable stories about my home and family with her. She said that she had often visualized what my home must look like from the stories I had shared with her. We were so pleased that she had been able to finally come down to visit us during Christmas of 2003.

Amelia talked about how much she would like to build one more house, and some of the plans she would include if she could rebuild. It was something she really enjoyed thinking about. As I began to reflect on those conversations we shared about her desire to build one more new home, I realized that during that same time her Heavenly Father was busy building that new home for her. I have wondered if Amelia had realized that she would soon be moving into a brand new home. *"In my Father's house are many mansions; if it were not so, I would have told you. I go to prepare a place for you. And if I go and prepare a place for you, I will come again and receive you to Myself; that where I am, there you may be also" (John 14:2-3).*

Building a new home can be a real challenge. There are so many decisions to be made. There is the frustration of contractors not showing up as promised, or not following through with your requests. There are months of patiently waiting for the finished product and hoping it will all turn out as planned. Amelia didn't have to deal with any of these challenges. *"Unless the Lord builds the house, They labor in vain who build it" (Psalm 127:1).* Her brand new home was designed and built by the Master Designer, the carpenter from Nazareth. Everything was perfect!

On Saturday morning when Amelia left us here, she went to live in this brand new home that had been prepared for her. *"This life is not all there is. Dying is not an end, but a beginning. Life on earth is just a dress rehearsal for our real life in heaven."* *(Amelia's Journal)* When Donna called at 1:10 a.m. to tell me what had happened, I'm really glad she did not say that Amelia had died. Instead, Donna said, "She's gone." I like to think that is a much better description of what transpired during those early morning hours of October 9, 2004. Amelia didn't really die. She just had to walk through the valley of the shadow of death (Psalm 23:4), in order to reach her final destination. Helen Keller said, "Death is no more than passing from one room into another. But there's a difference for me, you know, because in that other room I shall be able to see." In John 11:26, Jesus reminds us that *"Whoever lives and believes in Me shall never die."* Sir Walter Scott once poised the question, *"Is death the last sleep? No, it is the final awakening."* She fell asleep in this world and awakened in the presence of God. The Bible teaches that the soul of a believer in Christ goes immediately to heaven. To be absent from the body is to be present with the Lord *(II Corinthians 5:8).* The story of Lazarus and the rich man further confirms this teaching. *"So it was that the beggar died, and was carried by the angels to Abraham's bosom..." (Luke 16:22).* Abraham's bosom is a synonym for paradise, or heaven. I believe that a believer who leaves this life is immediately escorted by the angels of God into heaven to live with God, our Father, and His Son, Jesus Christ. Amelia immediately went to live in one of those many mansions in our Father's house. She no longer resides on Sand Hill-Shady Grove Road. Her new address is: *Heaven.*

Another wonderful transformation occurred with Amelia at that time. There is no more cancer, no more weakness, no more nausea, no more sorrow, or pain. *"And God will wipe away every tear from their eyes; there shall be no more death, nor sorrow, nor crying. There shall be no more pain, for the former things have passed away" (Revelation 21:4).* She has also been given the assurance of a perfect body! Our earthly body will ultimately be raised in glory and will be conformed to His glorious body. *"For our citizenship is in heaven, from which we also eagerly wait for the Savior, the Lord Jesus Christ, who will transform our lowly body that it may be conformed to His glorious body, according to the working by which He is able even to subdue all things to Himself" (Philippians 3:20-21).* As much as I miss my friendship with Amelia, I could not wish her back here with all the pain and suffering she endured during her last two years. Philippians 1:21 reaffirms, *"For to me, to live is Christ, and to die is gain."* Our emotions are selfish, and our focus is on our present loss. If we can just catch a quick glimpse of where Amelia is and what she is doing, we find solace. I am often reminded of a beautiful song written by Kim Noblitt when I attempt to catch one of these quick glimpses...

IF YOU COULD SEE ME NOW
Our prayers have all been answered, I finally arrived.
The healing that had been delayed has now been realized.
No one's in a hurry. There's no schedule to keep.
We're all enjoying Jesus, just sitting at His feet.
My light and temporary trials have worked out for my good.
To know it brought Him glory when I misunderstood.
Though we've had our sorrows, they can never compare.
What Jesus has in store for us, no language can share.
If you could see me now, I'm walking streets of gold.
If you could see me now, I'm standing strong and whole.
If you could see me now, you'd know I've seen His face.
If you could see me now, you'd know the pain is erased.
You wouldn't want me to ever leave this place,
If you could only see me now.

There is much interest surrounding the details of this awesome place called heaven. There are many differing opinions, interpretations of scripture, and unanswered questions. However, the Bible does give us some very specific details about heaven. One of the things that gave me great comfort during my initial days of profound grief after Amelia left us was to read about her new home. The final chapters of the book of Revelation give specific details about this place, this Holy City, that the Father has gone to prepare for those of us who are followers of Jesus Christ. A beautiful river runs through the city flowing out from the throne of God. Its water is crystal clear. The trees that line the banks of this river are the trees of life that bear twelve different kinds of fruit, a different one bearing its fruit each month. The walls of this city are made of shining jasper, and the foundations are of precious stones. There are twelve gates which are made of pearl. The streets are paved with pure gold. It is a very large city of twelve thousand furlongs square. There will be plenty of room for all who choose to live here for eternity.

Our words are certainly inadequate to describe how beautiful heaven must be. Our minds are incapable of comprehending how long eternity will be. *"But as it is written: "Eye has not seen, nor ear heard, Nor have entered into the heart of man the things which God has prepared for those who love Him" (I Corinthians 2:9).* Our perception of heaven tends to be that we know it is an awesome place, and we want to go there someday, but we're in no hurry to get there. Joe Louis once said, "Everybody wants to go to heaven, but nobody wants to die." I am reminded of a story I heard about a pastor who asked his congregation to raise a hand if they wanted to go to heaven. Everyone present raised a hand, except one man. The pastor was a bit perplexed by this, and asked the man if he wanted to go to heaven and why he had not raised his hand. To this the man responded, "Oh yes, I definitely want to go to heaven some day. I just thought you were getting up a load to go today!"

It seems illogical that we would desire to stay on this earth in our present state when we could have heaven. We live here in a world that is plagued by sin, worry, fear, heartache, disappointment, sickness, crime, abuse, famine, war, earthquakes, and other daily disasters, yet we have a longing to stay here. There are many reasons for this. We have been blessed with family that we love and do not want to be separated from them, even if it is only a temporary separation. We have goals we have set and desire to achieve them. We have tunnel vision for this day or this week, which makes it impossible for us to see the big picture that God has planned. We are looking with our physical eyes rather than our spiritual eyes. We see through tinted glasses now and can only visualize in part and not the whole. If we could truly catch a glimpse of where Amelia is and how well she is doing, we could not wish her back here for even a second. As I have grown older and friends and family members have moved on to their brand new home in heaven, there is a heightened interest and awareness of heaven. Yes, I do have friends and family whom I would not want to be separated from here. However, I must say that I do look forward to moving into my brand new home there someday.

I have chosen to be a follower of Jesus Christ. I have asked Him to forgive me of my sins and become the Savior and Lord of my life. Therefore, I have blessed assurance that Jesus is mine, and that one day, I will leave here and go to live in heaven for eternity. This means that I will see Amelia again. I am really looking forward to that. I used to talk with her daily, and I miss that so much. Meanwhile, I believe Amelia is looking down on us, and if we could hear her speak today, she might be singing one of her old choir songs, *Wait Till You See My Brand New Home.* What else is she doing there? She is enjoying spending time again with loved ones who went before her. Amelia loved her mother and missed her so much. What a joy it must have been to see her mother again!

Amelia is also spending a great deal of time praising God. She loved to sing, and she loved being a part of her church choir. As she became weaker and weaker, it became more difficult to see her in that state. When I remember the image of those last few days when she was so sick and so weak, I try to quickly erase that image from my mind. I replace it with an image I remember of Amelia one Sunday night as I visited her church and saw her singing in the choir. She was moving with the music, clapping her hands, and singing *Victory in Jesus!* She wasn't just singing it; she was daily experiencing it! It wasn't just a song; it was a reality for her. What joyful confidence she displayed that night. *"The LORD is my strength and my shield; My heart trusted in Him, and I am helped; Therefore my heart greatly rejoices, And with my song I will praise Him" (Psalm 28:7).* That is the way I like to remember her. That is what I believe she is doing today. *"But I will sing of Your power; Yes, I will sing aloud of Your mercy in the morning; For You have been my defense And refuge in the day of my trouble" (Psalm 59:16).* She is enjoying singing praises in the heavenly choir. She is singing *Victory in Jesus*, not just because she believes it, but because she has experienced the ultimate victory.

I also believe Amelia is looking down over us. *"Therefore, we also, since we are surrounded by so great a cloud of witnesses, let us lay aside every weight, and the sin which so easily ensnares us, and let us run with endurance the race that is set before us, looking unto Jesus, the author and finisher of our faith, who for the joy that was set before Him endured the cross, despising the shame, and has sat down at the right hand of the throne of God" (Hebrews 12:1-2).* In the first letter I ever wrote to Amelia, I described what we were going through as a race. I promised her that I would stand on the sidelines and cheer her on. Through the course of the race she ran with cancer, I tried to do that. Her race with cancer is now over. She may have lost that race, but the victory was won. *"I have fought the good fight, I have finished the race. I have kept the faith. Finally, there is laid up for me the crown of righteousness, which the Lord, the righteous Judge, will give to me on that Day, and not to me only but also to all who have loved His appearing" (II Timothy 4:7-8).* Amelia did indeed fight a good fight. She kept the faith until she finished the race.

Now the roles are reversed. She is now encouraging me to run with endurance the race that is set before me. She is now cheering me on, and I suspect that is not all she is doing. The first few weeks after she left us were so emotional for those of us who loved and missed her so much. Amelia made it clear to us all from the beginning of her battle with cancer that we were going to stay positive,

116

and we were not going to cry. I told Kim that I was sure she must be leaning over the rails of heaven when she caught us crying and saying, "No, no, we're not going to do that!"

I am not exactly sure where heaven is, but I know for sure that she is there. I do occasionally go to the cemetery where her earthly remains have been placed, but not because I think for one second that she is there. It just happens to be one of the places I can go to stir my thoughts and memories of the good times we shared, and rekindle the warmth that was ignited within my heart on the day we first met. I like to take her favorite flower, those sweet smelling gardenias, and leave them there. Everyone knew how much she loved gardenias, and I sometimes find that someone else has already left a bouquet there. On the day of the funeral service, Patty asked me to bring a bouquet of gardenias to the church. She placed them in Amelia's empty choir chair, as the remainder of the choir exalted Christ and honored her memory through music that day.

I continue to think often of the good times, and bad times that we shared. Yes, I still talk to her at times, and I often wish she could answer me. One such occasion was the first time I tried to repot the African violet she rooted especially for me. I know that African violets can be temperamental, and I surely did not want anything bad to happen to this one. I felt that she was watching over me intently and thinking, "She is going to kill it!" I just looked up and said, "Amelia, I sure wish you were down here right now doing this the correct way!"

There was an incredibly strong bond between Amelia and myself. It has been said that a friend is someone who reaches for your hand, and touches your heart. On the day that we first met, Amelia reached across the hospital bed and grasped my hand. Over the next two years, she touched my heart in an incredible way. It was a perfect friendship. The reason it was so perfect was because it was not devised by man, but ordained by God. He cannot do anything less than perfect. *"Every good gift and every perfect gift is from above, and comes down from the Father of lights, with whom there is no variation or shadow of turning"*

(James 1:17). We truly were best friends, confidants, and sisters by divine appointment. I miss her and all those special times we spent together. I'm looking forward to seeing her again one day when I move into my brand new home in heaven. We've got a lot of catching up to do!

Chapter Thirteen

IS THIS ALL THERE IS?

We now live in an imperfect world where no one is exempt from troubles. *"Yet man is born to trouble..."* *(Job 5:7).* *"Therefore do not worry about tomorrow, for tomorrow will worry about its own things. Sufficient for the day is its own trouble"* *(Matthew 6:34).* Amelia had endured the typical ups and downs this life has to offer. Although she could verbalize that her life had been good, she knew well what heartache and disappointment felt like. She had tried various means to meet the need these emotions had created.

Shortly after her divorce she became involved in a support group and remained active there for about five years. She related to me that it was during this time, and through this group, that she began a new pursuit of God. It was also during this time that someone shared a poem with her that became one of her favorites, and challenged her to move forward with her life. She had a framed copy of this poem in her home and called it to my attention one day while I was visiting with her. I read it with interest and amazement. The original author of this poem is debatable and unclear, but it clearly describes the life of Amelia...

COMES THE DAWN

After awhile you learn the subtle difference
Between holding a hand and chaining a soul,
And you learn that love doesn't mean leaning

And company doesn't mean security,
And you begin to learn that kisses aren't contracts
and presents aren't promises,
And you begin to accept your defeats
With your head up and your eyes open,
With the grace of a woman, not the grief of a child,
And learn to build all your roads
On today because tomorrow's ground
Is too uncertain for plans, and futures have
A way of falling down in mid-flight.
After awhile you learn that even sunshine
Burns if you get too much.
So you plant your own garden and decorate
Your own soul, instead of waiting
For someone to bring you flowers
And you learn that you really can endure....
That you really are strong
And you really do have worth.
And you learn and learn...
With every goodbye you learn.

Amelia realized that this life is full of troubles. However, she had become able to turn her adversities into learning experiences. She had made positives out of the negatives that had invaded her life. She had moved forward with her life, building news roads, and planting more gardens. She had learned that she was strong, and she really could endure. The acquiring of this knowledge would become invaluable in her future.

It was the year 2000, and we had all survived the feared transition into the new millennium. Things were going well for Amelia with her family and work. *"Isn't God amazing! Just when you think life is just where you want it, God comes along and changes things. I remember standing in my bedroom one day in 2000. It's like a moment frozen in time. I was standing in the middle of the room facing East. Why I remember that I can't tell you, but every time I recall that moment the way I was facing comes to mind. Someday I will know! I stood there and this question came to my mind. Is this all there is? There must be something more! I walked on through my room and didn't remember that moment again until a year later. God began to show me the something more." (Amelia's Journal)*

God does indeed have a perfect plan for our lives. He had known Amelia long before her birth (Jeremiah 1:5), and had designed a very special plan for her life. *"For I know the thoughts that I think toward you, says the Lord, thoughts of peace and not of evil, to give you a future and a hope" (Jeremiah 29:11)*. On that day in 2000 when Amelia had stood in her bedroom and poised the question, "Is this all there is?", she was beginning to recognize that there remained an unfulfilled need in her life. This is how she described it: *"By 2000, my daughter and her family had been attending the church for almost a year, maybe more by then. She had asked me several times to come hear their minister and hear their awesome choir. I was in my comfort zone! So while I was really interested (I love music and a good sermon) I didn't do anything for too long a while. When I finally made the decision (or God pushed me hard enough) to go, man, was I sorry I had waited so long! I didn't realize what I had been missing. I could see and feel the Holy Spirit in everything there. God knew just exactly where I needed to be. Something more is always coming! God used my child and her family to lead me there- to fill a longing that God had made me aware of on that day in 2000. When I knew I had found a church home was the day I remembered that day again. What an awesome God we serve! Something more is still coming." (Amelia's Journal)*

God knows our needs long before we begin to recognize them. He goes before us and is ever working things out for our good. That is exactly what He was doing for Amelia during this time. God knew that Amelia was about to face much adversity in her life. He knew she would need the love and support of her family. He knew they would all need the love and support of a loving and supportive church family. God was at work preparing the set for the events that were about to unfold on the stage of

Amelia's life. *"This life is not all there is. Dying is not an end, but the beginning. Life on this Earth is truly just a dress rehearsal for our debut in Heaven."* (Amelia's Journal) His plan is always perfect. His timing is always perfect.

Prior to January of 2002, Amelia had been in what she described and thought was her comfort zone. *"January of 2002 found me very satisfied, even happy, with my whole life. Work and my school family were great. We had settled in with our new principal and his assistant. God was working His plan."* (Amelia's Journal) Considering the events that were about to unfold in her life, it would not have been at all comforting for her to have remained there. It has been well stated that God loves us just the way we are, but He loves us too much to leave us there. *"God knew just exactly where I needed to be. Something more is always coming."* (Amelia's Journal) Something more was indeed coming!

"Haven't we all been there; whether it's a life-altering experience or just an everyday annoyance? We pray for it to just be over, and then we can go back to being thankful, but not while we're suffering- too much to ask of us. I believe that this is one of many messages that God has given to me and it has taken two years of living with cancer for me to really listen to Him. I believe that this is the message I hear today. God tells me to love the living- everything- everybody- whether you think of the circumstance or the person as good or bad. This life I have given to you. Be my faithful servant and when you get home, you'll be so happy to be with me. Nothing else will matter. All pain will be forgotten. You will have all you desire. Remember, I suffered and died on the cross just for you. I promised you a place of everlasting peace with me- No sadness, no sorrow, no pain- Just everlasting joy! Be ready for the day I welcome you home. Until then, show and tell others what living for me looks and feels like. Praise God, isn't that why we keep living- for the blessings the Holy Spirit gives us on earth and eternal life to come. Praise His name!! Give Him the Glory!" (Amelia's Journal)

God is omnipotent, omniscient, and omnipresent. He is able to stand in the middle of our life and see both sides. He could see

Amelia's past and know she was not going to be well prepared for her future. So he began to work in her present situation. Amelia had sat alone at home in what she thought was her comfort zone. God knew differently, and He began a good work in her life. He knew that something more was indeed coming, and He was the one working behind the scenes on the set at Amelia's school. Amelia would spend much of her day at school, and she would need much support and love. She would need to know there were co-workers who would be available to offer that encouragement, as well as a listening ear. It wasn't a coincidence that a godly man, who was also a pastor, had been sent to be the principal of that school. That was God at work!

God knew that when Amelia left school, she did not need to go home alone, slip back into that comfort zone, and wallow in loneliness and self-pity. God had begun to impress upon Kim that she should encourage her mother to get back into church. Kim did not give up and her persistence paid off. Amelia did decide to go to church one Sunday. Hearing the wonderful choir and sermon about Jesus Christ, the living water, was a long overdue and refreshing drink of water to her soul.

"In 2000, I would have told you that I clearly understood this prayer (that I had recited daily for 17 years) and had a good relationship with God. Mind you- I wasn't in church and had no fellowship with believers, but that was about to change. God was working out His plan in my life, as He is in yours. The something more for all of us is always in His plan. It comes in different ways and at different times, but it will come as we open ourselves to the Holy Spirit. Invite Him in!" (Amelia's Journal)

Just as our physical body demands attention, the soul also needs attention. Our body requires good nutrition, exercise, and rest to remain healthy. Our soul needs such things as fellowship with God, worship, meditation, and fellowship with other believers. Amelia recognized the needs of her soul. She had discovered that those things she had reached for and attained had not brought her the peace and happiness she had desired. She was beginning to realize that only Jesus could satisfy her soul. While her physical body was beginning to deteriorate, her soul was being renewed day by day. *"Therefore we do not lose heart. Even though our outward man is perishing, yet the inward man is being renewed day by day. For our light affliction, which is but for a moment, is working for us a far more exceeding and eternal weight of glory, while we do not look at the things which are seen, but at the things which are not seen. For the things which are seen are temporary, but the things which are not seen are eternal"* (II Corinthians 4: 16-18).

After Amelia returned to church and began to experience love and enjoy fellowship with other believers, it did not take her long to realize what she had been missing. *"BEHOLD, how good and how pleasant it is For brethren to dwell together in unity!" (Psalm 133:1).* She sensed a new safety and security, and she liked the way it felt. *"The name of the LORD is a strong tower; The righteous run to it and are safe"* (Proverbs 18:10). She had a new desire for the things of God, and she began to truly seek the Lord. *"And you will seek Me and find Me when you search for Me with all your heart. I will be found by you, says the LORD, and I will bring you back from your captivity..."* (Jeremiah 29:13-14). She often spoke of the regret she had of those wasted years in captivity. How she enjoyed being involved in worship, singing in the choir, having fellowship with other believers, and building a whole new circle of friends.

Amelia had been a great teacher to so many school students. It was during this time that she became a great student. She learned so much about the goodness and provision of God. She found it difficult to describe the great love, joy, and peace of God that she was experiencing. She stood in awe at the grace that was sufficient for every need. She was totally overwhelmed by the large band of angels that God sent to minister to her. She became intrigued with tracing that perfect plan of God and His hand on her life. She would often ponder the question she had poised two years earlier. She was overwhelmed at the something more God had brought into her life.

Amelia demonstrated a total confidence in God's providence. She had learned to place her trust in Christ alone, and He had well paved the way for the something more that she was now facing. *"God has a perfect plan for my life. Temporary setbacks should never disrupt my confidence that He will provide. Every aspect of my life has suffered a setback except the most important, and it has abounded. Spiritually, God has begun to show me the something more that I was missing. My desire is to have just a closer walk with Thee. My plea is that Jesus will grant this desire. We don't get to choose how it comes, and we don't have to be thankful for the pain, but with God's help, we can be thankful for the opportunity to use it for God's glory as a living testimony of His love and grace. As parents we want to provide our children with a good example of staying calm in the midst of crisis. Should I let cancer blind me to all the other blessings in my life?"* (Amelia's Journal) Amelia had come to realize that the adverse circumstances she was facing were an opportunity for finding God's faithfulness afresh, and sharing of His goodness and faithfulness with others. She was beginning to enjoy the fullness of the blessings that come to those who love God. *"BLESSED is the man Who walks not in the counsel of the ungodly, Nor stands in the path of sinners, Nor sits in the seat of the scornful; But his delight is in the law of the Lord, And in His law he meditates day and night. He shall be like a tree Planted by the rivers of water, That brings forth its fruit in its season, Whose leaf also shall not wither; And whatever he does shall prosper"* (Psalm 1:1-3).

Amelia did begin to use her situation to yield fruit for God's glory. She became a living testimony of His love, mercy, and grace. God's desire is that we respond to every adversity we face in a way that would glorify His name and point those who might be watching to the Savior. Amelia began to see the interruptions in her plans as opportunities for God to implement His plans. She learned much about the faithfulness of God. As her physical body grew weaker and weaker, her faith grew stronger and stronger. *"My flesh and my heart fail; But God is the strength of my heart and my portion forever"* (Psalm 73:26). She became confident that she could trust in Him and His divine plan for her. *"Trust in the LORD with all your heart, And lean not on your own under-*

standing; In all your ways acknowledge Him, And He shall direct your paths" (Proverbs 3:5-6). She found total peace and perfect joy because she had yielded herself completely to God. She had realized that in order to overcome, you must undergo. *"These things I have spoken to you, that in Me you may have peace. In the world you will have tribulation; but be of good cheer, I have overcome the world" (John 16:33).*

She could move forward with confidence, knowing that Christ was directing her path. She had become able to pray, "Not my will, but Thine be done." Her faith in His unfailing love sustained her. She had total confidence in God's faithfulness to carry her through every crisis. When the storms raged, she just remained calm, focused, and paddled a little harder.

It was Dwight L. Moody who described three different kinds of faith. There is struggling faith, which can be compared to a man floundering and fearful in deep water. There is clinging faith, which can be compared to a man clinging to the side of a boat. Then there is resting faith, which finds a man safe inside the boat, strong and secure enough to reach out his hand to help someone else. Amelia definitely had acquired this resting faith. Christ was at work in her life, transforming her into a person that was totally confident in her safety and security in Him. Her faith had become much deeper than her circumstances. She did not evaluate her situation with carnal reasoning, but with spiritual insight and trust in a God who could not fail her. *"THOSE who trust in the Lord Are like Mount Zion, Which cannot be moved, but abides forever. As the mountains surround Jerusalem, So the Lord surrounds His people From this time forth and forever" (Psalm 125:1-2).* She was leaning on the everlasting arms of God. They had been safe and secure enough to protect her from all harm. They were strong enough to give her the confidence she needed to reach out and help someone else. She continued to have that desire until the very end. When she realized she was too weak to attend the celebration service she had looked forward to, she wanted it to be held without her and verbalized, "It's not about me." Why did she do that? Because she wanted to reach out and help someone else. She was concerned about other people who would be there and did not have a personal relationship with her Savior. *"Something more is on the way."* *(Amelia's Journal)* Something more did indeed happen that night as nine people prayed and invited Christ into their lives. *"Something more is always coming."* *(Amelia's Journal)* Something more came less than two weeks later, as three more people prayed this same prayer at her funeral service. The prayer of David became an answered prayer in Amelia's life. *"Create in me a clean heart, O God, And renew a steadfast spirit within me. Do not cast me away from Your presence, And do not take Your Holy Spirit from me. Restore to me the joy of Your salvation, And uphold me by Your generous Spirit. Then I will teach transgressors Your ways, And sinners shall be converted to You"* (Psalm 51:10-13).

Looking back over the prayer she had prayed daily for seventeen years, I believe God was also faithful to answer that prayer in Amelia's life. Amelia had prayed, *"Lord, I offer myself to Thee, to build with me and do with me as Thy wilt. Remove the bondage of self that I might better be able to do Thy will. Take away my difficulties that the victory over them might bear witness to those I would help- of Thy love, Thy power and Thy way of life."* *(Amelia's Journal)* Amelia stepped out of her comfort zone and offered herself to Christ to do with her as He desired. He definitely had something more planned for her life. He ultimately did take away her difficulties, and the victory in Jesus she now enjoys has been a witness to others of the love, the power, and the way of life that Christ offers. What a tremendous testimony she was to all of us who knew her, of the goodness and sufficiency of God in times of need. Our lives are much richer, and our faith is much stronger because Amelia recognized that God had something more in His plan for her life, and she allowed Him to do a good work in her. *"Being confident of this very thing, that He who has begun a good work in you will complete it until the day of Jesus Christ"* (Philippians 1:6).

Amelia came to realize her real purpose in life. She was born to serve the Lord. She was made to praise and glorify Him. *"If anyone speaks, let him speak as the oracles of God. If anyone ministers, let him do it as with the ability which God supplies, that in all things God may be glorified through Jesus Christ, to whom belong the glory and the dominion forever and ever" (I Peter 4:11).* We may have only seen the tip of the iceberg in the something more God had actually planned through her life. We do know that at least twelve people professed faith in Christ during the last days of Amelia's life. Their lives have been changed for all eternity. Something more definitely awaits each of them. We know that countless others were strengthened and encouraged in their faith as they witnessed the strength, courage, and resting faith of Amelia during this storm in her life. May we all follow her lead, die to self, and let Christ reign supreme in our life, so that others who may be watching will discover that this is not all there is. There is more, so much more! *"Not that I have already attained, or am already perfected; but I press on, that I may lay hold of that for which Christ Jesus has also laid hold of me. Brethren, I do not count myself to have apprehended; but one thing I do, forgetting those things which are behind and reaching forward to those things which are ahead, I press toward the goal for the prize of the upward call of God in Christ Jesus" (Philippians 3:12-14).*

In my first letter to Amelia, I had compared her illness to a race. I had promised to stay on the sidelines and cheer her on to her victory. *"Do you not know that those who run in a race all run, but one receives the prize? Run in such a way that you may obtain it. And everyone who competes for the prize is temperate in all things. Now they do it to obtain a perishable crown, but we for an imperishable crown" (I Corinthians 9:24-25).* Many of us ran the race with Amelia and encouraged her to press on, but she was the one who would obtain the prize. There was infinite gain at the end of her race. Amelia obtained the crown that would last forever. Missionary Jim Elliot once said, "He is no fool who gives what he cannot keep to gain what he cannot lose."

On October 9, 2004, Amelia became able to forget all those things which were behind and started to enjoy all the things which are ahead for her as she begins eternity in heaven. She had pressed on through every crisis and storm she had faced. She had finally reached her ultimate goal. *"You will show me the path of life; In Your presence is fullness of joy; At Your right hand are pleasures forevermore" (Psalm 16:11-12).* She had finally discovered the ultimate something more!

≻Chapter Fourteen≺

CHOOSE YOU THIS DAY

Our attitude has a profound impact on our life. It was Winston Churchill who stated, "Attitude is a little thing that makes a big difference." We have a choice each day regarding the attitude we will take in matters that arise. The events that fill our lives are rather insignificant in comparison to how we choose to respond to those events. William James said, "It is our attitude at the beginning of a difficult task which, more than anything else, will affect its successful outcome." The choices we make have far reaching implications for us and all those around us. When we choose self-pity and negativism, we soon find that not only are we miserable, but those around us are as well. Attitudes truly are contagious. It has been well said, "When mama ain't happy, ain't nobody happy!" There certainly is some degree of truth to this statement. It is not very pleasurable to have to be around those who are never happy about any of their circumstances or situations.

We may be unable to control our situation, but we can control our attitude. Our circumstances may not change, but we can change how we respond to them. We can choose to be happy. Life is full of adversity, and we all face difficult circumstances. We have been reminded that while all things are not good, all things can work together for good, even in the midst of these bad situations we will face. Peter Marshall once said, "When we long for life without difficulties, remind us that oaks grow strong in contrary winds, and diamonds are made under pressure." God is truly able to cause unfortunate circumstances to work for good to those of us who love the Lord.

I believe there is a mental factor in fighting cancer. Patricia Neal noted, "A strong positive mental attitude will create more miracles than any wonder drug." It has been said, "Laughter is the best medicine." There are actually some physiological explanations for the truth in this statement. Proverbs 17:22 reminds us that *"A merry heart does good, like medicine, But a broken spirit dries the bones."* This positive attitude may not result in victory over the disease, but it can bring joy in the journey.

It has been well stated that " Situations don't make or break us. They just reveal who we really are." Everyone who knew Amelia observed her very positive attitude. I took her over to visit my parents one day. My mother immediately noticed Amelia's positive spirit and commented about how inspirational it was to be around her and see her optimism. Amelia verbalized that she could not imagine responding otherwise, stating, "No one would have wanted to be around me. I would not want to be around myself!" I spoke with our local gynecologist during Amelia's illness. He had also noted her positive attitude and commented, "If anyone can beat this thing, Amelia will do it!" Attitudes and outcomes are always affected by the choices we have made. Amelia's attitude was positive because she had chosen to be positive. Zig Ziglar stated, "You cannot tailor-make the situations in life, but you can tailor-make the attitudes to fit those situations." She had developed a supernatural joy that was not dependent on her circumstances. She had a sense of real security, knowing that she belonged to God, and He was in control. She knew that she could trust Him. She recognized that He was more capable of handling her circumstances than she was, and she had accepted His will for her life. *"Happy are the people who are in such a state; Happy are the people whose God is the LORD"* *(Psalm 144:15).*

We are all on a journey. We do not always get to choose the journey we may find ourselves on, but we can choose our ports of call along the way, and we can choose our final destination. We also can choose the attitude we will have along the way. Several years ago, a slogan became very popular and reminds us of the correct question we should poise in every situation. That question is simply, "W.W.J.D., What Would Jesus Do?" Our attitude should be the same as that of Jesus Christ. Our desire should become that in all things God would be glorified through Jesus Christ. We must learn to think and respond like Jesus. *"Let this mind be in you which was also in Christ Jesus" (Philippians 2:5).*

It was Brian Tracy who said, "You cannot control what happens to you, but you can control your attitude toward what happens to you, and in that, you will be mastering change rather than allowing it to master you." Amelia found herself on a long journey she did not choose to take. There were many destinations along the way from which to choose. It might have been easier to stop off and stay in those places called *Self- Pity* or *Discouragement.* However, she made a conscious choice not to go there. She chose to stay in places of *Hope* and *Courage.* She had chosen to be content in her situation, and she rested in the knowledge that God is faithful. She chose to view her present situation through eyes of faith. She could have inappropriately chosen to blame God and become angry. Instead, she chose to relax and bask in the sunlight of God's love. She could have elicited the sympathy of others by dwelling on her pain and the hardships she daily faced. Instead she chose to verbalize, *"It's not about me. It's all about Him."* *(Amelia's Journal)* What a difference she was able to make in the lives of others because of the choices she made for herself. She chose to let Psalm 34:1-4 govern her daily attitude. *"I WILL bless the Lord at all times; His praise shall continually be in my mouth. My soul shall make its boast in the LORD; The humble shall hear of it and be glad. Oh, magnify the LORD with me, And let us exalt His name together. I sought the LORD, and He heard me, And delivered me from all my fears."*

Cancer is a devastating disease by which all of us have been affected, either directly or indirectly. We have a choice in how we will respond to it. We can find positives, even in this negative situation. A very popular but anonymous poem has done just that...

WHAT CANCER CAN'T DO

Cancer is so limited...
It cannot cripple love.
It cannot shatter hope.
It cannot corrode faith.
It cannot eat away peace.
It cannot destroy confidence.
It cannot kill friendship.
It cannot shut out memories.
It cannot silence courage.
It cannot invade the soul.
It cannot steal eternal life.
It cannot quench the Spirit.
It cannot lessen the power of resurrection.

Cancer can do none of these things unless we choose to allow it to do these things. Life is indeed full of choices. Some of the choices are more far reaching than others. The most important choice we will ever have to make is poised in Joshua 24:15. *"And if it seems evil to you to serve the LORD, choose for yourselves this day whom you will serve, whether the gods which your fathers served that were on the other side of the River, or the gods of the Amorites, in whose land you dwell. But as for me and my house, we will serve the LORD."* This is the choice that carries eternal consequences. We must make the choice to walk by faith and serve the Lord. *"But without faith it is impossible to please Him, for he who comes to God must believe that He is, and that He is a rewarder of those who diligently seek Him"* (Hebrews 11:6). The old cliché is true: You are not ready to live until you are ready to die. *"Seek the LORD while He may be found. Call upon Him while He is near"* (Isaiah 55:6). If you have not already done so, I pray that today you will choose for yourself to serve the Lord. You'll be glad you did!

≻Chapter Fifteen≺

I CAN SEE MORE CLEARLY NOW

In 1972, Johnny Nash released his most popular hit, *I Can See Clearly Now.* In this song, he suggested that, because the rain was finally gone, he could now see the obstacles that had previously been in the way. Obstacles truly are opportunities to prove God's faithfulness. He will either make a way around them or give us grace to walk through them. There will continue to be obstacles and situations that we cannot fully see and understand until we see Jesus face to face. *"For now we see in a mirror, dimly, but then face to face. Now I know in part, but then I shall know just as I also am known" (I Corinthians 13:12).* I am also beginning to see more clearly now. There are still days when the weather forecast over my heart is "Partly cloudy with a few scattered showers." However, there are now more answers and fewer questions.

I truly believed that Amelia would receive a complete physical healing. On that first day that I met her, my last words as I departed her hospital room were, "I believe you are going to be all right." Her response had been, "I think so, too!" I daily claimed the promises found in God's word to this effect. I asked other prayer warriors to intercede for her healing. I know that people on at least three continents were praying specifically for her. We cried out to God and held out until those last days, believing He could still bring healing and hoping that He would. God heard those cries, and He answered our prayers. It's just that He had planned something much bigger and better for her. I recently saw a message board at a church that declared, "God's answers are often better than our prayers."

Amelia never asked us to pray for healing. She would always say, "Pray for strength." My prayers for physical healing were fueled by selfish emotions. That was what I wanted. I wanted to spend more time with her and be encouraged by her strong, resting faith. I wanted to go to Applebee's and have dinner one more time. I wanted to see her stand in the choir and sing *Victory In Jesus* once again. I wanted to take her to the beach and let her tender little feet feel the cool, soft, white sand. I wanted her to greet me at the door again with her big hug, and "I love you, love you, love you" routine.

I continued to plead with God, but things only seemed to get worse. I knew that God continues to have the power of physical healing, and I was disappointed that He did not choose this for Amelia. The one point I had not wanted to consider was that physical healing might not be in God's plan for Amelia. Proverbs 19:21 reminded me that *"There are many plans in a man's heart. Nevertheless the Lord's counsel- that will stand."* This became another of those times in my life when I had to respond on the basis of what I knew, rather than how I was feeling. I was reminded again of the vast contrast between my finite knowledge and the infinite wisdom and power of God. I also remembered that He was aware of my distraught feelings, He was very near, and was concerned for me. *"The Lord is near to those who have a broken heart"* (Psalm 34:18). In fact, He was so concerned about my heartache and disappointment that He kept all my tears in a special bottle. *"You number my wanderings; Put my tears into Your bottle; Are they not in Your book?"* (Psalm 56:8).

God's ways are not our ways. His plans are not our plans. I believe His desires became Amelia's desires quicker than we realized. She had realized that He was more to be desired than all she would leave behind. She counted everything as loss compared to knowing Him (Philippians 3:8). I was amazed that she never asked us to pray for healing. I was surprised that she rejected the proposal to be involved in clinical trial drugs that might possibly have helped her. She had no desire to explore any alternative approaches that were mentioned to her. We had talked about everything; everything except the fact that her health was rapidly declining, and she was not going to make it.

I've wondered many times why she never talked about dying. Was it because she had made it clear that, "We're not going to cry"? Was it because she sensed that my tender heart was breaking? Was it because God had indeed given her sufficient grace and perfect peace that was totally beyond our ability to understand?

Donna and I discussed this on several occasions. We concluded that Amelia had experienced a deeper relationship with an all-sufficient God and had begun to move to a higher plane. She had been totally overwhelmed by God's grace and goodness. She had experienced a foretaste of glory divine, and it was so awesome that she couldn't look back. She had sought the Lord and found Him to be everything she had ever needed and more. John Bunyan stated, "In times of affliction we commonly meet with the sweetest experiences of the love of God." God's love, mercy, and grace had totally captured her heart. She had decided to follow Jesus, and there would be no turning back. She had been given a little glimpse of where this incredible journey was taking her, and she liked what she saw. *"For I consider that the sufferings of this present time are not worthy to be compared with the glory which shall be revealed in us" (Romans 8:18).* She had become totally submissive to Christ and was able to confidently say, "Have Thine own way, Lord!" She had become able to pray as Christ had prayed in Mark 14:36, when He said, *"Abba, Father, all things are possible for You. Take this cup away from Me; nevertheless, not what I will, but what You will."* She may not have fully understood His plan, but she accepted His control over her life. She suffered quietly and kept her focus on her eternal destiny. All was well with her soul.

I recently had lunch with Kim and Donna. I shared with them that day that I had really believed in my heart, and thought in my mind, that Amelia would be healed. Kim responded, "So many people prayed that prayer; it obviously was just not God's will." God does instruct us to pray for healing, but we are also instructed to seek God's will. *"Now this is the confidence that we have in Him, that if we ask anything according to His will, He hears us" (I John 5:14).* We can find numerous accounts in the Bible in which people prayed for healing. Some of these people received immediate healing, and some did not. We are taught in Luke 22:42 to follow Christ's example and pray that God's will be done. Our hearts are beginning to find a safe and peaceful refuge in the knowledge that God's will was done. We are all beginning to see more clearly now.

Initially, I went through the typical emotions associated with grief. Time is on our side when we deal with these issues. Losing a loved one is something from which you never fully recover. Seeking to understand God's will and accepting His plan have helped a great deal in the healing process. I have come to understand that it is okay to grieve, and it is okay to grieve in my own way. In fact, it is healthy and necessary that I grieve in my own way. Nobody knows how I feel. People told me they knew what I was going through because they had lost a close friend. Everybody and every situation is different, and every relationship is different. Nobody truly knew exactly how I felt. I had even become concerned that I was not handling my grief very well. Then one day, several months after Amelia's passing, I watched an interview with Dana Reeve (widow of Superman's Christopher Reeve) on The Oprah Winfrey Show. She suggested that the way you deal with grief is to grieve. Grief is normal and healthy. It is a necessary component of the recovery process.

I began to contemplate Kim's statement again. If physical healing was not God's will, then what had God's will been in all of this? Most people are guided by their physical senses. In doing so, we are unable to see the big picture, the perfect plan God has designed for our lives. We must use our spiritual senses to see the things of God. We must learn to *"...walk by faith, not by sight"* (II Corinthians 5:7). Our goal is to enjoy a good life here that is free of heartache and pain. His goal is that in our lives He would be glorified, and others would see the goodness of the Lord.

Sometimes, God doesn't seem to be faithful because He doesn't answer our prayers the way we desire. I really believed Amelia would be healed. She was much too young to die. She had so many things left that she wanted to do. Things were going well with her life. She was happy with family, work, and church activities. This was the Amelia I saw with my physical eyes.

It isn't so difficult to trust God when all is well. The true test comes when the strong winds begin to blow, and we find ourselves in the eye of the storm. Like Peter, we begin to doubt that God is going to be faithful to see us through our difficult circumstances. We begin to question His perfect plans. It is important in these times that we quickly recognize and deal with the source of our doubts and fears. *"For God has not given us a spirit of fear, but of power and of love and of a sound mind"* (II Timothy 1:7). Only Satan would try to convince us that God is not kind and loving. These thoughts are devised by the deceiver in an attempt to make us lose our focus. As we take our eyes off Christ, the source of our strength, our faith becomes weak, and we begin to lose our joy. We become weak and vulnerable. We begin to doubt or question God. The good news is that we can defeat Satan and his tactics through the power that is within us. *"You are of God, little children, and have overcome them, because He who is in you is greater than he who is in the world"* (I John 4:4). We must learn to keep our thoughts on the goodness of God. *"Finally, brethren, whatever things are true, whatever things are noble, whatever things are just, whatever things are pure, whatever things are lovely, whatever things are of good report, if there is any virtue and if there is anything praiseworthy, meditate on these things"* (Philippians 4:8). God's desire is that we respond to every situation we face in this life in a way that would glorify His name and point those who may be watching to the Savior.

We must learn to strengthen our spiritual senses and keep our spiritual focus. We must remember that God is far too wise to ever be mistaken. He is the omniscient God, the all-knowing God. He is the God who can see our past, our future, and make wise decisions for our present situation. We can only see our present situation, but God sees the complete picture. We can make plans for today or tomorrow, but God is working out His eternal plan. We have only very limited knowledge to glean from in making important decisions. God is all-seeing and all-knowing. He possesses infinite wisdom and always knows what is best for us. God chooses for us what we would choose for ourselves if we were capable of seeing from the beginning to the end. *"He has made everything beautiful in its time. Also He has put eternity in their hearts, except that no one can find out the work that God does from beginning to end" (Ecclesiastes 3:11).* He cannot make a decision that is less than perfect. It is impossible for Him to miss something that is going on in our life. *"Are not two sparrows sold for a copper coin? And not one of them falls to the ground apart from your Father's will. But the very hairs of your head are all numbered. Do not fear therefore; you are of more value than many sparrows" (Matthew 10: 29-31).* If he never misses a sparrow that falls to the ground, then surely He watches over you and me. We would be foolish not to trust His decisions. How blessed we are to be children of this omniscient, omnipotent, and omnipresent God. He is incapable of making less than the perfect decision for us in every situation we face.

God is also much too loving to ever be unkind. His love is a perfect love, for God is love. How much does He love us? *"For God so loved the world that He gave His only begotten Son, that whoever believes in Him should not perish but have everlasting life" (John 3:16).* His love is an everlasting love. Nothing can ever separate us from this perfect and everlasting love of God. *"Who shall separate us from the love of Christ? Shall tribulation, or distress, or persecution, or famine, or nakedness, or peril, or sword? As it is written: "For Your sake we are killed all day long; We are accounted as sheep for the slaughter." Yet in all these things we are more than conquerors through Him who loved us. For I am persuaded that neither death nor life, nor angels nor principalities nor powers, nor things present nor things to come, nor height nor depth, nor any other created thing, shall be able to separate us from the love of God which is in Christ Jesus our Lord" (Romans 8:35-39).*

God cares too much for us to ever mistreat us. He bids us to come to Him with our concerns and lean on Him. *"Come to Me, all you who labor and are heavy laden, and I will give you rest. Take My yoke upon you and learn from Me, for I am gentle and lowly in heart, and you will find rest for your souls" (Matthew 11:28-29).* He has not forgotten about us during our times of adversity. He has promised He will never leave us nor forsake us. In Matthew 28:20, He reminds us, *"I am with you always, even to the end of the age."* In Isaiah 49:16, God again reminds us that He has not forgotten us. *"See, I have inscribed you on the palms of My hands..."*

I suppose the most asked question in times of adversity has been, "Why would a loving God allow such a horrible thing to happen?" God is able to look at the total picture with perfect love and infinite wisdom. He knows that our time on this earth is limited. *"And as it is appointed for men to die once, but after this the judgment, so Christ was offered once to bear the sins of many. To those who eagerly wait for Him He will appear a second time, apart from sin, for salvation" (Hebrews 9:27-28).* He also knows that we were born into trouble and sin. We have all made many mistakes. *"As it is written: "There is none righteous, no, not one" (Romans 3:10). "For all have sinned and fall short of the glory of God" (Romans 3:23).* God knows that sin leads to death. *"For the wages of sin is death, but the gift of God is eternal life in Christ Jesus our Lord" (Romans 6:23). "Then, when desire has conceived, it gives birth to sin; and sin, when it is full-grown, brings forth death" (James 1:15).* We are God's creation. We were made to fellowship with Him. Sin separated us from God. He loved us too much to leave us in our hopeless, helpless condition. *"For whoever calls on the name of the LORD shall be* saved" *(Romans 10:13)*. Amelia had called on His name and had been given the assurance of eternal life. *"And this is the testimony: that God has given us eternal life, and this life is in His Son. He who has the Son has life; he who does not have the Son of God does not have life. These things I have written to you who believe in the name of the Son of God, that you may know that you have eternal life, and that you may continue to believe in the name of the Son of God" (I John 5:11-13).*

God could certainly have given Amelia the gift of physical healing. He has all power over heaven and earth. He was more than capable. However, He was also capable of looking into her future. There would have been more pain, more suffering, more heartache, more adversity, and ultimately death. It was His infinite wisdom and perfect love that influenced His decision to bypass a temporary healing and give her the ultimate healing. He always desires our eternal best over a temporary fix.

God has made a way for us, where there otherwise would have been no way. We have to look no further than Calvary to see the perfect love He has for each of His children. It is at Calvary that we find healing for the soul. It is at Calvary that we find forgiveness and salvation. Calvary is our only hope for our helpless condition.

After we have accepted this free gift of salvation that was purchased with a price most precious at Calvary, God surely has something more planned for our lives. He has commanded us to go and tell this good news to others. *"But you shall receive power when the Holy Spirit has come upon you; and you shall be witnesses to Me in Jerusalem, and in all Judea and Samaria, and to the end of the earth" (Acts 1:8).* Amelia came to realize that God had something more planned for her life. We can only imagine what He saw as He stood in her present situation and gazed into her future. Perhaps He saw people in her workplace who needed to have an opportunity to minister to one in need. We come in contact daily with people who are hurting and need love, support, and encouragement. We are often too busy to even recognize the needs of those with whom we spend the most time each day.

Maybe He saw co-workers who were also dealing with pain and illness and had wanted to give up. Amelia's courage was contagious. She may have given someone there a renewed courage and faith.

Perhaps He saw people in her church who needed to be challenged or encouraged. Maybe there were those who had grown tired in doing good. *"But as for you, brethren, do not grow weary in doing good" (II Thessalonians 3:13)*. There may have been some who were weary and discouraged in their soul. *"For consider Him, who endured such hostility from sinners against Himself, lest you become weary and discouraged in your souls" (Hebrews 12:3)*. Someone needed to remind them to persevere in doing good. *"And let us not grow weary while doing good, for in due season we shall reap if we do not lose heart. Therefore, as we have opportunity, let us do good to all, especially to those who are of the household of faith" (Galatians 6:9-10)*.

He may have seen people seated in the doctor's office or the infusion center who had lost all hope. Perhaps Amelia's living hope and positive attitude in the midst of much adversity gave them a new hope and courage to press on in the midst of their storm. He must have also seen people like me who needed a new friendship, a new opportunity to encourage and be encouraged, and to see again the hand of God at work orchestrating His perfect plan for our lives.

I'm sure he also saw the faces of those twelve special friends and family members who had not yet professed faith in Christ for their salvation. He knew this would be a perfect opportunity for them to witness the profound difference He was making in Amelia's life during her time of need. They would be able to see how He had calmed the raging storms in her life. If they could see the peace, joy, love, hope, strength, and courage she had to press on, they would surely want to invite Him to be the Lord of their life. He knew they would attend the special services planned for her and would be given the opportunity to make that decision.

God looked across Amelia's future and saw these great needs. He recalled a question He had poised to Isaiah many years ago about who He could send to accomplish the task at hand. Isaiah responded affirmatively to this divine call before God had even revealed to him what the task would involve. Once again, God poised this same question. Then He recalled the prayer Amelia had prayed daily for seventeen years. *"Lord, I offer myself to Thee, to build with me and do with me as Thy wilt. Remove the bondage of self that I might better be able to do Thy will. Take away my difficulties that the victory over them might bear witness to those I would help- of Thy love, Thy power and Thy way of life"* (Amelia's Journal). Amelia did not know what the task was that God had planned for her as she had prayed that prayer many years earlier. What she was really saying was, *"Here am I. Send me."* It seemed like another one of God's perfect plans, as Amelia had willingly offered herself to Him, to be used according to His will. He did indeed remove the bondage in her life, so that she became better able to seek and do His will. He ultimately did take away her pain, suffering, and difficulties. *"Many are the afflictions of the righteous, But the LORD delivers him out of them all"* (Psalm 34:19). The victory she conquered over them has been a tremendous witness to all of us, of God's love, His power, and His way of life. The prayer she had prayed daily for seventeen years had finally been answered. God had chosen her for a mission. She answered the call, and served Him well.

Countless lives were forever changed because Amelia willingly said, "Here am I. I offer myself to Thee." We will never know the vast impact she made through her living testimony of God's faithfulness. Only God will be able to make an accurate assessment of all the good things that came from this seemingly difficult situation. To God be all glory for the great things He has done!

God did not cause this adversity in Amelia's life. God is all-powerful, and He could have certainly stepped in and prevented this illness from ever inflicting her body. *"...Salvation and glory and honor and power belong to the Lord our God!"* (Revelation 19:1). However, God does allow things to happen in our lives to give us the opportunity to grow more into the likeness of His Son.

He provides opportunities for us to be His mirror, reflecting His love and grace for others to see. *"But we all, with unveiled face, beholding as in a mirror the glory of the Lord, are being transformed into the same image from glory to glory, just as by the Spirit of the Lord" (II Corinthians 3:18).*

He doesn't even ask us to be thankful for everything that comes our way. He does, however, ask us to be thankful in everything. *"In everything give thanks; for this is the will of God in Christ Jesus for you"(I Thessalonians 5:18).* Brian Tracy has suggested that you should "Develop an attitude of gratitude, and give thanks for everything that happens to you, knowing that every step forward is a step toward achieving something bigger and better than your current situation." Amelia had developed this attitude of gratitude. She had a thankful heart, and this is why she never had a reason to complain. It is His desire that we use every situation in our lives to glorify His name and point others to our Savior. *"For you were bought at a price, therefore glorify God in your body and in your spirit, which are God's" (I Corinthians 6:20).* We are God's prized possession, purchased through the giving of His only beloved Son.

It has been said that hindsight is 20/20. We can look back on our past, but we are incapable of looking ahead and seeing God's perfect plan for our future. This may be the reason we have concerns, face fears, and ask questions about what God is up to in our lives. It is our tendency to fear the unknown. We do not have to worry and fear what our future holds. We can rest in peace knowing that God holds our future firmly in His hands.

What I had wanted was not the thing that would best glorify God and fulfill His plan for all the people who were touched by Amelia's faith. Now that I can see more clearly, I have changed my wants. I want Amelia to enjoy being in the presence of the Lord. I want her to enjoy being free of pain and suffering. I want her to enjoy her reunion with her loved ones in heaven. I want her to enjoy singing in the heavenly choir. I want her to meet me one day at those pearly gates and give me a big hug and say, "I love you, love you, love you" again.

Eleanor Roosevelt once said, "Many people walk through our lives, but only a few leave footprints on our heart. " My life is much richer because Amelia touched it. It is forever etched with special memories of the times we spent together. I hope that I am a stronger person because of the life lessons I learned on my journey with her. I started this journey with a clear call from God to love and encourage Amelia. Today, I am a different person because of the love and encouragement she gave to me. I may never fully understand why God chose me to take this incredible journey with Amelia. I do know from past experiences that my biggest storms have been sent to grow me and better equip me for the next storm I will face. I have learned that something more is always coming.

Amelia taught me so much about how to live and how to die. She reminded me of how blessed I really am, even on my worst day. Through my journey with her, I learned that God does indeed have big plans for our lives, and this short life here is merely a preparatory phase for the real life He has prepared for us. I believe God's ultimate desire for each of us is *"...That where I am, there you may be also" (John 14:3).* She taught me that God is always a step ahead of us and is always working things out for our good. *"But may the God of all grace who called us to His eternal glory by Christ Jesus, after you have suffered a while, perfect, establish, strengthen, and settle you" (I Peter 5:10).* He will never call us to a mission that He does not equip us to accomplish.

Through it all, I have learned to trust in His unfailing love. I have learned that I can depend upon His word, and all of His promises are true. I have learned that *"To everything there is a season. A time for every purpose under heaven: A time to be born, And a time to die..." (Ecclesiastes 3:1-2).* I have learned that *"A good name is better than precious ointment, and the day of death than the day of one's birth" (Ecclesiastes 7:1).* I have learned that life is indeed fragile, and we are not promised tomorrow, so we should live each day as if it were our last. I have learned that God can take our biggest tragedies and turn them into

145

our greatest triumphs. I have learned that our purpose in this life is to learn to love and trust God and to show His great love to others. I have learned that even when I do not understand His plan, I can always trust His heart and His perfect plan for my life. I have learned that every event that happens in this life is orchestrated by a loving, gracious, and faithful God. It is not dependent upon my approval, but it is always designed with my best interest in mind. I have learned that the Lord is on my side, and I will always be on the winning team. I can't lose, for winning! *"If it had not been the LORD who was on our side, When men rose up against us, Then they would have swallowed us alive. When their wrath was kindled against us; Then the waters would have overwhelmed us, The stream would have gone over our soul; Then the swollen waters Would have gone over our soul. Blessed be the LORD, Who has not given us as prey to their teeth. Our soul has escaped as a bird from the snare of the fowlers; The snare is broken, and we have escaped. Our help is in the name of the LORD, Who made heaven and earth" (Psalm 124:2-8).* I am becoming more impressed by His plans, and am finding it easier to pray, *"Thou will be done."* I am discovering that He really is much more capable than I am of knowing and meeting my needs. I am now totally convinced that God truly does do all things well!

I have learned the importance of searching for the positives when we find ourselves in negative situations. I am becoming better able to see the silver lining amidst the stormclouds. Genesis 50:20 states, *"But as for you, you meant evil against me; but God meant it for good, in order to bring it about as it is this day, to save many people alive."* God truly took something that was meant to harm Amelia, made many good things come from it, and brought the assurance of eternal life to at least twelve people during this difficult situation.

I have learned that there will continue to be tough questions. I have learned the answer to those tough questions is simply that God is faithful. We can always trust Him. God was faithful to supply all of Amelia's needs according to His riches in glory by Christ Jesus. Amelia was faithful until death to Him as well. God has different goals, plans, and purposes for each of us. However, His ultimate goal for us all is that in the good times and the bad, we would glorify Him in our lives. I have no doubt that Amelia was greeted in heaven with the commendation of "Well done, good and faithful servant. Enter into the joy of your Lord." I recall again the conversation that we had on the day that I first met her. I told her that I believed everything was going to be all right and she agreed. Everything with Amelia is now all right. She ran a courageous race, and she did indeed finish well. *"The Lord gave, and the Lord has taken away; Blessed be the name of the Lord" (Job 1:7).* "Amelia, I've got to go now. I love you, and I'll see you again soon!"

EPILOGUE

The day following Amelia's funeral, Donna and I returned to her home to assist Kim in packing away some of Amelia's possessions. It was a very painful but therapeutic process, giving us some closure during this time of loss and grief. Donna called me into Amelia's bedroom and told me to sit down and take a break. She had found Amelia's handwritten journal that I have shared with you in this book.

As we sat in the bedroom floor reading this and wiping away our tears, I had to ask myself the same question she had poised. "Is this all there is? There must be something more." I felt as though I was at a crossroads in my journey. I had lost my traveling companion. Where would I go from here? I had told Amelia on several occasions during her illness that I was going to write a book about our journey. I felt immediately that this was indeed the next phase of the journey for me. This book has been my next "something more."

One of my favorite stories is *The Starfish Story*. This is a very popular and motivational story that was written by Loren Eiseley. It reminds us that we really can make a difference. Many versions of this story have been told, but the message remains the same. As the story goes, there was a person on a seashore just before the sunrise, who was frantically trying to toss all the starfish that had washed ashore back into the water, so that they would not die in the heat of the day. This person was approached and questioned about the fact that he was wasting his time, as he could not possibly make a difference in the task he had undertaken. There were far too many starfish on miles and miles of beaches. His response, as he tossed another starfish back into the water, was that he had made a difference for that one!

We have all been touched by a diagnosis of cancer in some way. If you have been directly affected by it, I pray this book will encourage you, and Amelia's strong faith and courage will be contagious. If you have a friend or family member who is fighting this battle, I pray this book will encourage you to become one of their angels sent to minister to them in their time of need. There are many people all around us who are suffering and need hope and encouragement. The task may seem overwhelming. People often disappear from the lives of the terminally ill, because they don't know what to say or do. You don't necessarily have to say anything, just be there. Sometimes our presence speaks louder than our words. Just be available, and God can use you to minister to those in need. He is more interested in your availability than your capability. You may be the person He has specifically chosen to make a difference in another person's life. Mother Teresa once said, "If you can't feed a hundred people, then feed just one." I challenge you to find that one person and get busy. It has been well said that you may be only one person in the world, but you may be the world to one person. Romans 15 admonishes us to be encouragers to those who are weak. We are to bear the burdens of others and glorify God together.

Now that I have completed another phase of my journey, I find myself at yet another crossroads. Again, I must pause and ask myself, "Is this all there is?" Again, I am sure of the answer. There must be something more!

— —

During Amelia's illness, I begged, pleaded, and even tried to bargain with God as I prayed for her healing. "Lord, just let Amelia get well, and we will certainly use this experience to glorify Your name and tell others about the amazing things You have done." God did answer my prayer exceedingly abundantly above what I had asked of Him. Amelia received the ultimate healing, because His will was done rather than mine. Therefore, I must do the things I promised God I would do.

Amelia also loved to hear me tell the story of how we met. She would often introduce me to a friend, and then she would say, "I want you to tell our story!" She wanted everyone to know all the details about those God ordained plans that had brought us together. Not only must I do the thing I promised God that I would do, but I also cannot disappoint Amelia. Therefore, I must continue to tell our story.

- -

Luanne is available to speak to church and civic groups about her experiences on this journey that she shared with Amelia. By sharing Amelia's story of faith and courage, others will see that they can turn tragedy into triumph. Luanne also desires to heighten ovarian cancer awareness and give women important information about this "disease that whispers". Her message could be life-changing and life-saving. She can be contacted at: somethingmorebk@yahoo.com. Her mailing address is: P. O. Box 249, Franklin, GA 30217.

SYMPTOMS OF
OVARIAN CANCER

A feeling of being bloated

Vague abdominal and pelvic discomfort

Gastrointestinal symptoms such as gas, nausea, indigestion,

constipation, or diarrhea

Back pain and fatigue

Unexplained weight loss or gain

Frequent and/or urgent urination

Menstrual disorders, or pain during intercourse

Most of us have experienced some of these symptoms at one time or another, and they are usually not considered to be life threatening. However, if they persist for several weeks and typical means of intervention do not resolve the problems, further investigation into the etiology of these symptoms should be pursued. Ovarian cancer has been referred to as "the disease that whispers", or "the silent killer", because the symptoms are usually vague and mimic other less serious conditions. Unfortunately, the disease has often become more advanced and spread to other vital organs, which produce the identifying symptoms, before it is correctly diagnosed.

An annual Pap smear is very important for the detection of cervical cancer, but it is NOT an accurate test for ovarian cancer. If you have any of the above symptoms that persist after short term traditional treatment, you should see your doctor and ask for three tests that may help spot a problem early: a vaginal/pelvic exam, a pelvic sonogram, and a CA 125 blood test. EARLY DETECTION CAN MAKE ALL THE DIFFERENCE!

According to the American Cancer Society, Cancer Facts and Figures 2005, there will be 22,220 new cases of ovarian cancer in the United States in 2005. There will also be 16,210 estimated deaths from ovarian cancer in the United States in 2005.